Five-Star
LIVING
on a Two-Star
BUDGET

Margaret Feinberg
Natalie Nichols Gillespie

HARVEST HOUSE PUBLISHERS

EUGENE, OREGON

Scripture quotations are taken from The Message. Copyright © by Eugene H. Peterson 1993, 1994, 1995, 1996, 2000, 2001, 2002. Used by permission of NavPress Publishing Group.

Cover by Terry Dugan Design, Minneapolis, Minnesota

Cover photos © John A. Rizzo/PhotoDisc Green/Getty Images; Comstock Images/Getty Images; James Lauritz/Digital Vision/Getty Images; Comstock Images/Alamy; Ingram Publishing/Alamy; Steve Allen/Brand X Pictures/Alamy; Brian Hagiwara/Brand X Pictures/ Getty Images

FIVE-STAR LIVING ON A TWO-STAR BUDGET
Copyright © 2006 by Margaret Feinberg and Natalie Nichols Gillespie
Published by Harvest House Publishers
Eugene, Oregon 97402

Library of Congress Cataloging-in-Publication Data
  Feinberg, Margaret, 1974–
  Five-star living on a two-star budget / Margaret Feinberg and Natalie Nichols Gillespie.
       p. cm.
  ISBN-13: 978-0-7369-1677-6 (pbk.)
  ISBN-10: 0-7369-1677-6
  1. Shopping. 2. Deals. 3. Generosity. I. Title: 5-star living on a 2-star
budget. II. Gillespie, Natalie Nichols III. Title.
  TX335.F44 2006
  640'.73—dc22   2005018049

Printed in the United States of America

  06 07 08 09 10 11 12 13 14 / BP-CF / 10 9 8 7 6 5 4 3 2 1

★★★★★ Contents ★★★★★

★★★★★

The Five-Star Living Approach

Everybody loves a deal—whether you are living on a modest income or a six-figure one. We are no exception. One of us is a mom and stepmom of seven who constantly strives to stretch the family budget beyond where it should be able to go. The other is a newlywed and first-time home buyer who is facing all of the financial challenges of just starting out. Self-proclaimed bargain hunters, we love to find a sale and share our good fortune. But the tips and tidbits that we have included from our research and life experience are meant to do more than just pad your pocketbook. They are designed to free up your dollars so you can make a bigger difference in the world.

In *Five-Star Living on a Two-Star Budget*, you will be given quick tips and helpful hints on everything from makeup and fashion freebies to saving money on the purchase of a home or car. You will discover beauty tips, rebate secrets, and ways to manage all those money-saving devices. You will also find suggestions on ways to invest your time and talents. The goal is to help you lower your stress levels, enjoy life, and save money while affording you the opportunity to live like you already do—or even better—and use your savings to benefit those around you.

Five-Star Living isn't about being tight or cheap. It's about learning how to enjoy great restaurants, fine hotels, and the activities you love while staying within your budget.

Remember, the best things in life—kisses, sunsets, and walks on the beach—are still free. The next-best things in Five-Star Living come with a price, but remember, it is almost always negotiable!

Disclaimer

The only thing more fun than finding a great deal is letting everyone else know about it so they can enjoy the same benefits. We have done our very best to compile some of the latest-and-greatest tips and insider secrets so that you truly can experience Five-Star Living on a two-star budget.

Please note that some of the companies, stores, and websites mentioned may have undergone changes by the time you pick up this book. Some will move, transition, or close their doors. Many of the companies we mention will change their prices and promotions—eliminating some of the ones we describe and introducing new ones. We can't guarantee that everything you read will still be available. Our hope is that within these pages you will find the valuable tools you need to start digging up deals of your very own.

By listing a particular company or product, we are by no means endorsing their business practices or policies or the products. We just think we have discovered some great ways to track down the best life has to offer—and some screamin' deals you really need to know about.

Our goal with this book is to share our best so that you can live your best. Read on, and here's to Five-Star Living!

The Live It! Give It! Principles

If you had to choose a hotel between one and five stars and price was not a factor, how many stars would you choose? Duh! Five stars, baby, all the way. Right? Most people would pick the five-star hotel, especially if they weren't picking up the tab. Why? Because a true five-star hotel offers comfort, ease, and all kinds of amenities. It provides visitors a level of quality above its competitors. Simply put, a five-star hotel is the best.

So what would happen if you could take the five-star concept and turn it into a five-star lifestyle? What if you could take some of the things you learned from the temporary lap of luxury and bring them into your daily life? Is it possible to permanently experience a five-star lifestyle? We think so!

True Five-Star Living brings joy. Not the ecstatic Look-at-me-I-just-got-a-new-Coach-bag! kind of momentary glow or the I-just-spent-the-day-at-the-spa kind of temporary relaxation, but a deep-seated peace and satisfaction that lasts a lifetime. Five-Star Living isn't about the fancy resort you booked on Expedia or the Tiffany bracelet you found at half price last year. Five-Star Living is about elevating your living standard within your means to the highest quality, not just materially, but also spiritually, physically, and emotionally. True Five-Star Living won't drive you into debt; it will drive you out of debt. It won't leave you with so many things that you can't open your front door; it will leave you surrounded by high-quality items you appreciate and enjoy. It won't leave you frazzled on an endless search for more; it will give you a sense of contentment at having just the right amount. And it doesn't just feel good; it also involves *doing* good. Real Five-Star Living is a life well lived, not just for yourself but for others too.

You don't need a Donald Trump-sized income to experience a full and generous life. In the following pages, you are going to learn how to live big on only a little. You'll discover ways to become a savvy shopper and find out how a little time and research online and in your own community can save you big bucks—money that you can use to benefit those around you and still enable you to live a better quality of life.

Those who experience true Five-Star Living operate under what we have dubbed the "Live It! Give It!" principles: God gave you everything you have, so it really belongs to him. You honor him when you manage well what he has given you (Live It!). He blesses you when you share what he has given you with others in need (Give It!).

Our premise is pretty simple: If you spend less money to achieve the same or an even higher standard of living, then you will enjoy life more and can afford to save and give more.

If you choose to apply the Live It! Give It! principles to your life, you will find them to be more fulfilling and satisfying than chasing down this season's Fendi or trying out the trendiest restaurants. The key to real Five-Star Living is being wise with what you have been given, multiplying it, and then sharing everything you can with others. That is the way to unleash the formula for experiencing joy.

How do you get started? By beginning to examine your big picture and create a budget of your money, your time, and your talents. You can even pull out a sheet of paper and begin making notes on where your resources are going.

In the area of time, *ask yourself these questions (and answer them honestly!):*

★ *How is my time being spent?*

★ *Where do the hours of my day go?*

★ *Do I have an organizer or chart that records where I am spending my time?*

★ *Are there any ways I could be spending my time better?*

★ *Do I enjoy where I spend my time?*

★ *Is my time better spent in more productive endeavors?*

If you head out the door for work each morning with a feeling of dread, chances are you are not spending your time wisely. Ideally, your life's work should allow you to use your talents and enable you to pursue your passion. If your job or lifestyle prevents you from doing either, then you're more likely to become bored, frustrated, burned out, or stressed out.

If you are not doing what you feel called to do, ask yourself how that could change. Even if you can't change jobs right away, begin taking steps toward a new career. You may need additional training or classes, but with a little determination you can make a change. In the meantime, look for ways to use your talents and pursue your passion outside of work. Volunteer. Start a side business. Get involved in your community.

When you reflect on the way you spend your time, you may discover that you need to make some practical changes. You may need to turn off the TV or unplug the Xbox. You may need to develop healthier ways to de-stress at the end of the day. Or you may need to make time for an activity such as exercise or spending more quality time with friends.

Five-Star Living also means building "retreats" into your daily schedule where you can refresh yourself mentally, emotionally, and spiritually. Some of these retreats may be momentary deep breaths or walks outside. Others may include reading, prayer, or even shopping. Longer retreats include vacations or weekends away with friends. True Five-Star Living demands that time be spent on you. It is not selfish for you to take care of yourself, and that includes spending time doing things you love with the people you love. It will renew your overall energy and enthusiasm for life.

In the area of money, *ask yourself these questions:*

★ *Do I need a money makeover?*

★ *Do I need to learn some new savings techniques?*

★ *Is my debt out of control or causing myself or my loved ones stress?*

★ *Do I shop wisely, getting the most quality and quantity for the resources I have to spend?*

★ *Is all of my disposable income being spent only on myself and those I love, or am I helping anyone else?*

If you are constantly worried about money, studies show you are at risk for many ailments and crises, including a depressed immune system, psychological and marital problems, career problems, heart attacks, anxiety, strokes, suicide, diseases—and here is an interesting one—double the risk of gum disease! Go figure.

Five-Star Living means taking a hard look at where your money goes and figuring out ways to spend, save, and give more efficiently. Five-Star Living does not mean giving up your comfortable lifestyle. It means enhancing the value of your purchases so that you can still enjoy what God has given you and return the favor by giving to others. You can reduce your debt, buy things you love, and save for the future. Great money management takes time and effort, but it will vastly improve your quality of life.

In the area of your talents, ask yourself questions like these:

★ *What did I love to do as a child? Do I still love those things?*

★ *How am I using the gifts God has given me?*

★ *In what ways am I exercising my talents and honing my skills?*

★ *How are my talents and skills being used to bless others?*

★ *Am I doing the things that fulfill me, are the right fit, and give me feelings of peace and satisfaction?*

People were created with unique purposes and will feel the best spiritually, mentally, emotionally, and physically when they are doing what they are designed to do. Using your talents is not selfish; it's what you were made for. If you love to paint, buy some canvases, brushes, and paint and go to town! If animals are your passion, raise them or volunteer at a local humane society. If you love to help people, plug into a local ministry or community organization where your talents can be used.

Remember that no one else in this world can do exactly what you can do in exactly the same way. You have things to contribute that no one else can. Develop those gifts, talents, and skills, and exercise them often. If you sing, sing in places other than the shower. If you dance, dance with abandon. Your enthusiasm and passion will draw others like a magnet, and they will want to know your secret. Then you can introduce them to the fruits of Five-Star Living, because the benefits of Five-Star Living are many—reduced stress levels, enjoyment of life, a renewed appreciation for family and friends, discovery of new places, and an overall satisfaction that you are living your best life.

When you settle for a one- or two-star existence, you miss out on many of the good things life has to offer. By taking steps to lead a five-star life, you will be able to eliminate some of the stress-inducing factors in your life, secure in the knowledge that you are investing your time into more of what is truly important, spending money more wisely, and using your talents and skills in ways that bring satisfaction and joy. Five-Star Living, here we come!

Action Points

The Live It! Give It! Principles

★ Forget the feeling that you have to accept a substandard quality of life in order to prove you are wise in your spending.

★ Give graciously and even sacrificially to others as part of your five-star standard.

★ Avoid being wasteful and impulsive in your spending.

★ Learn new techniques and methods for savvy shopping.

★ Be willing to put in the time required to find good deals.

★ Spend wisely on items of quality.

★ Invest first and foremost in relationships.

★ Aim for a five-star emotional, spiritual, intellectual, and physical life.

Managing Your Methods

Okay, we can hear you asking, "Where do I start?" Or protesting, "There's no way I can live a five-star life on my income." We think you can, and we're here to get you started. In order to live a five-star life, a life that is peaceful, fulfilled, and balanced, you have to get organized. It takes a little (sometimes a lot) up-front work to get your finances in order, debt under control, "giving gene" activated, and your own filing system developed.

Wait! Don't put this down now. We promise you can do it! Just stick with us, and you'll find out how easy it is to get a big picture of the lifestyle you want to lead, and how to begin on the income you already have—no matter how small or big.

The first thing we have to talk about is money. A lot of it is about the money, honey. No getting around it. If you want to be able to lie down at night without tossing and turning about the bills, you are going to have to get your finances in order. That includes an activity that most people try to avoid: budgeting. The good news is that when we talk about five-star budgeting, we aren't suggesting that you learn to live without the things you love. Instead, we want to encourage you to spend on the things you adore while trimming away those things that rank as not-so-great. As actress Julia Roberts said in *Steel Magnolias*, "I'd rather have 30 minutes of wonderful than a lifetime of nothing special."

Wouldn't you?

Successful budgeting begins by realizing what money really means to you. Money buys more than just material objects. For some people, money buys significance or security. For others, it buys power, acceptance, or self-esteem.

What does money mean to you?

This is one of the most important questions you'll ever come across because it exposes the motivation behind the way you spend. You may be compelled by issues that you have never considered.

It's also important to reflect on what your family taught you about money. Some parents raise their children with an open checkbook—exposing every financial windfall or crunch that the family experienced. Other parents choose to keep their finances sealed tightly so that the children never have to be concerned. Many parents are somewhere in between in their philosophy and teachings.

No matter how much or how little you knew about your parents' actual financial situation, you grew up watching their spending habits. Was your mom or dad particularly loose or tight in their spending? Were your parents divorced, single, or remarried; and was money ever a sore spot? Odds are that the way your parents raised you has a tremendous impact on your financial situation today. It is important to recognize their influence—both good and bad—and embrace the healthy habits while rejecting those that may undermine financial stability.

The bottom line is that if you are in debt and you want out, you are going to have to change your spending behavior. For five-star spenders, that means a balanced diet of spending that will change habits for a lifetime, just as a food diet should. If you are so strict that you allow yourself nothing pleasurable in your spending or eating, your "diets" are doomed to fail. Instead, strike a healthy balance and aim to stay there.

It's All in the Budget

Learning how to budget is actually pretty simple. Budgeting simply means making sure that your expenses don't exceed your net income. If you don't know where your money is going, then it's impossible to know whether you're living within your means. That's why it's important to spend a month collecting all your receipts in an envelope, shoebox, or folder.

To figure out your income vs. expenses, you'll need:

- a pen
- a notebook
- a calculator
- a copy of all your receipts, including checkbook stubs or bank statements and credit card bills

Begin by creating categories for your expenses. These may include:

- Tithe/giving
- Savings
- Professional expenses (travel, clothes, work-related meals not covered by your company, memberships, subscriptions)
- Housing/utilities (mortgage or rent, home owner's insurance and taxes, cable, Internet, satellite TV, electric, water, sewer, gas, etc.)

- Transportation (car payment, insurance, repairs, and auto club membership)

- Food (groceries and eating out)

- Insurance (health, life)

- Health (doctor bills, prescriptions, dental work, eyeglasses, etc.)

- Entertainment (movies, video and DVD rentals, CDs, skating, skiing, sports events, concerts, etc.)

- Travel

- Gifts (birthday, Christmas)

- Miscellaneous (dry cleaning, household supplies)

Record your expenses under each heading and total the amount. Now compare the figure to your income after taxes. If you are spending more than you are making, then you need to find ways to cut back. Can you add another roommate? Cook at home? Cut out excess cable channels? Rent movies rather than go to the theater (or at least avoid the expensive snacks while you are there)? You need to find ways to cut back so that your extra money won't be going toward servicing debt.

One way to always know exactly where your money stands is to have someone tutor you on Quicken or Microsoft Money, software programs that will automatically keep track of your spending and all of your accounts, as well as separate your purchases into categories, providing you with charts and graphs and making income taxes a cinch. The trick to these programs is that you need to get a receipt for everything (and we mean everything) you purchase every day. Each evening, take a few minutes to enter those receipts into your program, and voilà! Your accounting is all done.

If you already have your spending-to-income ratio under control, and you are making more than you spend, then it's time to evaluate what is truly important to you. Where do you want your extra money to go? A portion should go to beef up your savings—whether it's for a major purchase like a car, college for the kids, a new home, or retirement. But the other portion is where Five-Star Living comes into play.

You might consider putting extra money aside as your dream fund. What have you always wanted to do? Where have you always wanted to go? Do you want to buy a new computer or techno gadget? Would you like to be able to afford to take some time off of work and pursue a personal hobby or passion? Would you like to volunteer or take an outreach trip somewhere in the world? By saving ahead of time for your five-star dream, you'll be able to make it come true sooner than you think.

> **Live It!**
>
> Even if your bills are on auto pay, you should always review your monthly statements to check for excess or erroneous charges.

Getting Out of Debt

If fulfilling your five-star dream seems out of reach because of debt, don't be discouraged. You can get out of debt. Stories abound of people who have been able to climb out of tens of thousands and even hundreds of thousands of dollars of debt.

We know. We've climbed out of the debt trap ourselves. Your basic motto should be: Where there's a will, there's a way.

While visiting Alaska one summer, I* met the man of my dreams. We began dating, and within a few months it became obvious to both of us that this relationship was for keeps. There were only two problems. The first was that he lived in Alaska, a place I never wanted to consider living full-time. The

---

* Rather than saying "I (Margaret)" or "I (Natalie)," we decided to just use "I" for both of us to keep things simpler. We've included information about each of us on the "About the Authors" page at the back of the book.

second was that my new love had about $17,000 of debt—student loan debt, which is actually considered "good" debt by financial experts because it is debt acquired to help you get ahead—but still debt. After a lot of prayer and some encouragement from my mom, I decided I would give Alaska a try and discovered I could actually survive the winters.

The debt was another story, a bigger hurdle than the darkness and rain that plagues southeast Alaska. We agreed we wouldn't get married until he was debt free. He decided to leave his job at an airline for a far better paying job with the federal government. He moved in with his parents. He bought a ten-year-old car. This guy was serious, and it showed how much he really loved me.

He cut back on lots of extras and began renting movies instead of going to the theater, cooking in rather than eating out, and buying simpler gifts during the holidays. Meanwhile, every free dollar went to pay off the student loan debts (and a simple but beautiful wedding ring). One year later—and approximately two weeks before our wedding date—he received the final notice from Sallie Mae. The loans were paid in full, and "he" became "we." Within a month after our marriage, we received a letter from the same financial institute inviting us to apply for another low-interest loan. We promptly shredded it.

My husband and I are convinced that going into marriage debt free was one of the best things we have ever done. It has prevented countless conflicts and lots of stress. When we look back, it seems incredible that he was able to pay off that much debt in one year. But when you are disciplined and determined, anything is possible.

So make it your goal to get out of your credit debt and pay back as many loans as you can. It takes determination and sacrifice, but if you can learn to live on less you can become debt free (with the exception of "good debt," meaning real estate or educational loans that increase your net worth

or ability to earn more). Depending on how many companies you owe, you may want to talk to a debt consolidator
about combining your debt into one payment. These types of
financial advisors will often negotiate with credit card companies and other businesses to knock down your interest
payments and any excess fees.

If you're determined to get out of debt without a financial
advisor, then you need to consider two schools of thought
on debt reduction. Some advisors recommend that you focus
on the highest-interest debt and pay that off first. It makes
the most fiscal sense, but it doesn't work for some people
because the size of the loan is so discouragingly large. That's
why a second group of financial advisors recommends that
you pay off the smallest loan first even if it's not set at the
highest interest rate. They believe that, like dieting, even a
small success delivers a significant amount of satisfaction. So
paying off one loan will provide the incentive and motivation to pay off more and serve as a reminder that becoming
debt free is possible. Only you know your personal motivation style, so choose the plan that works best for you.

For financial coaching from an organization with integrity,
visit Crown Financial Ministries, *www.crown.org,* for free articles, budgeting guides, and live advice online from a trained
budget coach. Crown also has trained volunteers around the
country to coach you out of your financial messes. The best
part: It's absolutely free. Call (800) 722-1976 to find out if
there are volunteers in your area.

If you think getting out of debt means all work and no
play, think again. Look for ways to provide yourself with
little incentives and bonuses along the way so that you will
stick to your budget. Paying off a particular credit card obviously shouldn't be rewarded with a no-holds-barred shopping extravaganza at Neiman Marcus, but that doesn't mean
you can't enjoy a reasonable purchase or treat! Rewarding

yourself will help you stay strong for the journey of becoming debt free.

You may also want to get in the habit of giving yourself and your spouse an allowance—an amount of money you can use to buy anything you want each week. If you're in a heavy reduction mode, you may want to limit this to $10 or $20, but if you have more disposable income, you may want to increase this amount to reflect your standard of living. Your allowance can be used on anything that allows you to enjoy a five-star life. For some, that may be as simple as having the house stocked with a name-brand soda or fresh flowers. Others may choose to use their allowance to eat out or go to a movie. You may save up your allowance for a trip or a larger purchase. Having money you can freely spend—even if you have other financial limits—will help you stay on the road to a five-star, debt-free lifestyle.

> ### *Live It!*
>
> Do you have a weakness for spending money? Are there certain items that you can't help buying or certain stores or shopping areas that make you naturally want to spend more? If you are trying to save money or get out of debt, you need to recognize your weaknesses. Be aware of particular impulse items that you're tempted to buy. Unless you are financially secure and want to give away some things, skip purchasing what you already have several of, even if it's on sale.

Once you are used to seeing where your money goes and you have a budget you can live within, you can relax a little. Start examining a different aspect of your finances from time to time. You may spend one month reflecting on your fixed expenses, such as house, car, and utilities, to see if there's anything you can reduce. You may spend another month tracking the amount of money you spend eating out. Another month you may examine your work-related expenses. By focusing on one area at a time, you can hone your budget to a figure that truly works for you and your lifestyle.

Saving for the Future

A crucial part of maintaining a five-star lifestyle is learning how to save. It's more than just about retirement or finding a quiet community to live in and play golf when you are 65. Savings help relieve stress and pressure during life's transitions. Whether you are changing jobs, careers, having a baby, or just need to take a sabbatical, savings give you breathing room in life.

One of the first places to tuck money is your IRA (Individual Retirement Account). You should talk to a financial advisor about whether a traditional IRA or a Roth IRA (which allows greater flexibility) is better for you. An IRA will allow you to invest several thousand dollars annually tax free or with deferred taxes, allowing your money to grow more quickly. If you maxed out your IRA for the year (because there is an annual limit), then you should consider other financial options, such as bonds, stocks, money market accounts, and other investments, that can allow your money to grow on its own. Generally, investments with higher yields result in larger potential gains, but they are also accompanied by greater potential losses. That is why it's important to diversify your savings and investments. It's worth contacting a financial advisor to help you plan for your future.

That's So Taxing

In addition to budgeting and saving, you need to make sure your taxes are in order. Depending on your lifestyle, whether you are married or single, and whether you are self-employed, you may have a simple or complex tax form to fill out in the spring of every year. If you don't feel comfortable with your tax forms, then by all means hire an accountant with a good reputation. An accountant may cost you a few hundred dollars each year, but the service is well worth the extra expense. Not only can an accountant help you find extra deductions and make sure you get a full refund, but also good accountants are insured, so if they make a mistake they will cover the difference. That's a benefit worth paying for every year!

Four Tips to Choosing a Tax Preparer

1. Know your tax preparer's specialty. Ask potential accountants what types of clients they usually work with and what types of forms they usually fill out. If your tax preparer specializes in bookkeeping instead of taxes, hire someone else.

2. Know what kind of service you expect. Depending on your personality, you may prefer a tax preparer from a nation-wide company, such as H&R Block, or you may prefer a local specialized firm. Choose the type of business that feels comfortable to you. After all, it's your money.

3. Research the tax preparer's reputation. Always ask around for referrals among friends, family, and co-workers. Beware of any tax preparer who manages to get extraordinary refunds for their clients. You don't want to work with anyone who is dishonest.

4. Ask the tax preparer how many forms they expect to submit to the IRS on your behalf. If they are filling out a long form, ask if a simpler form can be used. Remember that the less paperwork, the less cost to you.

Saving Begins Now

Saving begins with the small stuff. Saving a few bucks here or there may not seem like much, but you would be amazed at how quickly it can add up. Coupons and rebates may seem like foreign territory, but if you are serious about getting the most out of every dollar, it's time to learn how to speak this new language, especially if you have a family to buy for.

With seven kids, we buy a lot of household cleaners, health and beauty items, and food staples, all of which have frequent rebates and coupons. The first trick of the trade is to get the Sunday newspaper and take out the coupons and store advertisements. I prefer to cut the coupons right away; but if time is short, I take them with me in the car and carry scissors in my purse. When I am waiting to pick up kids from school or even sitting at a long red light, I will clip a few coupons and file them. Yes, file them in a small plastic file.

The second step to saving money with coupons is to develop a system for filing them and making sure you have it with you at all times. If you don't have the coupons where you can find them easily when you are standing in the checkout line, coupons will be more frustration than benefit.

Live It!

Choose a filing system that works for you, and clip coupons from each Sunday's newspaper. If there are very good deals in one week's paper, you can sometimes get extra copies of the coupon inserts at your local newspaper office. As you file them, pull out any that have expired and throw them away.

Coupon organizers come in a variety of shapes, sizes, and materials, from leather-look organizers to clear plastic sleeves and from canvas pouches to cardboard pocket files. One site, *www.organize-everything.com,* offers a $4.99 coupon organizer that velcros to the grocery store cart so that you can quickly flip through all your coupons. I use a poly envelope with tabbed pockets, and I have labeled the tabs in the same order that products are shelved in the grocery store I frequent most. For example, my front tab is dedicated to meats, produce, and dairy. The next pocket is bread and breakfast items. Next is beverages, followed by frozen items, and then cans. You may choose to file your coupons alphabetically or by expiration date. Filing them by aisle makes it simplest for me to find them when I need them.

For fastest shopping, clip only the coupons for products you regularly use and weed through your file for expired coupons before you shop. If you have more time, clip coupons for items you don't need if the coupon makes the item free or nearly free. In that case, buy the products with the goal of donating them to local organizations in need. Find out if any grocery stores in your area double or triple coupons, either on a regular basis or on a single day each week. This savings can add up quickly, and it might be worth making a drive of some distance once a month or so to use coupons to receive virtually free products before the coupons expire.

There are plenty of coupons available for more than just groceries. Visit *www.entertainment.com* and find out if there is an Entertainment Book for your area. The books are $20 to $30 annually and include hundreds of coupons for grocery stores, restaurants, travel, professional sports tickets, local arcades, dry cleaning, oil changes, concerts, and theater, plus national store coupons from places like Target, New York & Company, Claire's, and more. Entertainment Books also include coupons for discounts on theme park tickets and rental cars, and they offer great deals on hotels. If you know you will be traveling to a city in another state for even a few days, an Entertainment Book for that city can pay for itself several times over in dining and activity savings. If a book isn't available for your area, consider buying one for a place you might visit, if only to use the national deals and travel offers.

Give It!

Do you have a cabinet full of hotel soaps, shampoo samples, extra toothbrushes, and other items you don't need? Consider filling shoeboxes with these items, plus school supplies, small toys, and candy for the Samaritan's Purse Operation Christmas Child program. Each fall, Samaritan's Purse collects filled shoeboxes for its Operation Christmas Child program and distributes them to children in need around the world. Visit *www.samaritanspurse.org* for more information.

As soon as I can, I thumb through the weekly ads, especially the grocery stores, local drugstores like Walgreens, and chains such as Target, Wal-Mart, Office Depot, Best Buy, and Staples. I quickly circle or highlight any sale items I know I need, plus any good deals or rebates that catch my eye. If I know I have a coupon for the item as well, I may note that on the ad with an asterisk or by simply writing the word "coupon" so that I will remember to pull the coupon out. Some friends I know pull out the coupons they will use and paper clip them to the store ads. I carry these ads in my car during the week for quick reference when I get the chance to stop at those stores. Some weeks I never make it to the store and end up throwing the ads away. But the weeks when I have the time and money to shop, I am always glad to have the ads already marked so that I can use my time efficiently in each store.

If you hate making multiple stops, find out which stores in your area match prices or accept competitors' coupons. If you have the competing store's ad with you, it's a cinch to buy the sale items from both places in one stop. Just put the items on sale at the other store in your cart, and when you check out tell the cashier that you want to "price match" them. Show the clerk the ad from the other store and the sale items you've chosen, and the cashier should be able to take it from there. Be aware that items must match exactly—brand, size, and weight—and that most stores do not match buy-one-get-one-free promotions or percentages off the price.

Before you head out, take a quick check online for any additional savings. Did you know that there are websites where you can print out for free or even buy the coupons you need? Also check the paper, store ads, and in-store brochures for any rebates being offered. Decide whether the products you would have to buy are worth the rebate item or the money back for the time and effort invested in an envelope and stamp. If they are, buy them. With rebates, I often keep the forms at the very front of the coupon pouch rather than in their respective categories so as not to forget what special items I want to buy. When you get ready to pay for your items in the store, ring the rebate items separately so that you have a separate receipt that can be mailed in. Remember to take UPC codes off the packages of items that require them for the rebate right when you get home so you don't forget and throw the UPC away when you open the item.

If you have a small copier at home, it is well worth making a copy of your form, receipt, and UPCs and jotting down the date you mailed the rebate request in. Keep these rebate proofs in a basket or drawer and throw them away when you receive the rebate. That way, if you do not receive a rebate within the appropriate time frame, you can contact the company to make sure they received it. If they did not, you can then fax, mail, or scan and e-mail your copy in; and companies will usually give you the benefit of the doubt and get your rebate processed.

Watch for grand openings of new stores in your area, as stores often give away free products or offer great deals to get customers used to coming in. When the CVS drugstore chain bought the Eckerd drugstores in Florida, CVS spent three weeks giving away tons of free products in order to gain customer loyalty. The stores gave customers $25 gift cards to transfer prescriptions and printed coupons for free items in their flyers that included free greeting cards, store-brand items, cosmetic items, digital photos, and more, plus buy-one-get-one products galore. By transferring prescription refills for each of seven family members, I had $175 in free gift cards, plus at least $100 in free merchandise. Deals like that don't come along often, but when they do, take advantage of them.

When you are in stores, a general rule of thumb is to head toward the back to find the clearance items. Checking through them is a good idea, but beware of being tempted to do too much impulse buying. If clearance items can be put to use as gifts or will definitely be used by your family, great. If you want to buy them to give away, fine. But don't grab 14 dented cans of chicken chili or 47 pairs of black shoelaces for ten cents each unless you are sure you know someone who will use them. If they don't get used, they are not a good deal—no matter how low the price. Stock up on holiday decorations right after the holiday, when discounts can range from 50 to 90 percent off, and look on endcaps in stores like Target and Wal-Mart to find the marked-down merchandise. If you find great gift items or small toys and trinkets, stock up if you have a place to store them so that you always have birthday party or shower gifts on hand.

> ### Live It!
>
> I have a drawer in one file cabinet we have dubbed the "prize drawer." It is filled with pencils, small toys, candy, cosmetics, and other items I have found for usually 50¢ or less. When a child has behaved particularly well or gotten a good grade on a tough test, a trip to the prize drawer is in order. It's great positive reinforcement and well worth the few dollars' investment.

When you want to save time, shop when no one else can. When most people are at work in the middle of the weekdays, grocery stores may be nearly empty. Late at night is also usually less busy. If you want to be a good steward of the time you have, try to avoid shopping between 4 PM and 6 PM on weekdays, and as much as possible during weekend days and Sunday evenings. Also, plan ahead for holidays so that you are not standing in line for a turkey on the day before Thanksgiving or trying to buy your holiday punch and last-minute gifts on December 24.

Action Points

Managing Your Methods

★ Think about what money means to you and what motivates your spending habits.

★ Set up a budget, and make sure you're sticking to it.

★ If you need help with your debt, hire a reputable financial advisor or someone who works with debt consolidation or consult *www.crown.org* for free financial tools and advice.

★ Begin saving for the future—whether it's through an IRA, investments, or other savings.

★ Make sure you are using a good tax preparer.

★ Begin clipping coupons and develop a system for organizing them.

★ Look for rebate forms and take advantage of them. Gather receipts and UPC codes as soon as you get home from the store, and place them in an envelope right away so that you won't forget to get them in the mail.

★ Photocopy rebate forms and proofs of purchase.

★ Look for markdowns and clearance items on endcaps and at the back of stores.

★ Avoid peak shopping times, such as after school and work and the day before holidays.

★ Keep items you found at a bargain on hand for birthday, shower, and teacher gifts.

Beauty Bargains and Fashion Flair

The devil wears Prada, but all you can afford is Payless. You like Gucci, but lately you've been shopping at Goodwill. And you would love to have a Kate Spade bag, but the closest that you can get is a knockoff. You're not alone. The good news is that you can upgrade your appearance without emptying your pocketbook. All it takes is a little fashion sense, some fashion investing, and a few beauty products to make you shine.

Fashion Flair

If you don't have a huge income, then you are going to have to make some smart investments to find the right high-flying fashion pieces you need. Obviously, it would be wonderful to be decked from head to toe in couture, but you're going to have to make some choices about what to buy on a budget. A name-brand coat, shoes, and purse are smart investments because they are distinctive pieces you'll be able to wear regularly and enjoy. Something like a white T-shirt—whether it's made by Ralph Lauren, Diesel, or Old Navy—is still just a plain shirt, so choose your accent pieces wisely.

Once you've decided what you are looking for and the brands you want to wear, it's time to begin shopping. When you are spending hundreds (and even thousands) of dollars on an item, you want to find classic pieces that will stand the test of time. For the most part, avoid that hot pink, floral-patterned skirt that is so trendy this spring but so *out* by fall. Choose perennially classic colors and prints that still make their own splash.

> ### Give It!
>
> Do you have professional attire that is collecting dust in your closet? Consider donating it to Dress for Success, *www.dressforsuccess.org.* This nonprofit organization helps low-income women as they transition into the workforce. Each client receives one suit for job interviews and a second suit when they land the job.

You can visit chichi stores like Hermes or Chloe between seasons and find considerable savings. Retailers such as Nordstrom and Neiman Marcus also offer nice clearance prices. Another option for saving money on high fashion is to look for stores that specialize in selling clothes that are last season. Large retailers, including Filene's and Loehmann's, sell designer clothes such as Marc Jacobs and Stella McCartney at a discount. Filene's also has famous discount stores called Filene's Basement, *www.filenesbasement.com,* in Atlanta, Boston, and New York City.

Small retail stores also specialize in offering couture at big discounts. Luxe, *www.luxeatlanta.com,* is a 5000-square-foot store in the Buckhead area of Atlanta that features so-last-season designer clothes at 50 to 80 percent off the original retail price. If you live in the area, take advantage of their sales. It's like Saks Fifth Avenue without paying the Saks price.

In the Midwest states of Oklahoma, Texas, Arkansas, Missouri, Kansas, and Nebraska, the NBC chain, also known as Name Brand Clothing, *www.nbcclothing.com,* warehouses literally tons of off-season and slightly damaged clothing and accessories at rock-bottom prices. While you may have to spend some time searching through the racks for your treasure, when you pull out that DKNY top for 99¢ that is only missing a button, you will feel as though you have struck gold.

Discount stores aside, some of the best prices on five-star fashion can actually be found online. Two websites that every fashion diva should bookmark are Bluefly, *www.bluefly.com*, and Designer Outlet, *www.designeroutlet.com*, which offer discounts on clothes and accessories. A recent Helen Wang pink brocade rounded collar blazer was $239.20 on Bluefly—marked down from $500. An Armani velvet scarf was priced at $75 at Designer Outlet—reduced from $180. Both offered more than 50 percent savings on the original retail price.

Five-Star Quote

"I'm a black-belt shopper, always have been...I still get a little thrill whenever I see these two words: free and discount."

—Oprah Winfrey

★ ★ ★ ★ ★

In nearly every city there are chains of discount stores that offer high-end department store brands and an occasional couture item at a fraction of the price. Marshalls, T.J. Maxx, and Ross are some of the more popular ones, and each offers special enticements to keep shoppers coming in. Some have their own credit cards that offer additional rebates or discounts for shopping in the store; most offer seniors an extra discount one day each week. (If you are over 55, enjoy!) Even these stores have to make way for new merchandise, so off-season sales are the best times to enjoy discounts off the discounts. If Gap, Limited, Express, Ann Taylor, Liz Claiborne, and DKNY are your faves, these stores are a great place to start.

Outlet malls began popping up 20 years or so ago, and many across the country are still going strong. The idea is that companies open their own discount stores to move past-season items, returns, and slightly damaged goods at rock-bottom prices. However, some of the prices are not so rock-bottom, and the same items could be obtained at a good sale at Macy's or Nordstrom. The trick is to know the retail prices in order to determine if you are getting a good deal on those Nine West shoes. So get educated about the look you are trying to obtain. Go online to the high-end department store and couture websites and take a look at the retail prices of some of your favorite items. Note the current colors and styles. If you are fashion challenged, ask close friends what their recommendations would be for you. Once you are armed with the right information, you will be a wise consumer, able to sift through all the merchandise and make great choices on where to spend.

> ### Live It!
>
> Part of getting the most out of a five-star life is to incorporate your favorite fun things with your favorite friends. If you want to hit the outlets but they are an hour's drive away, make a day of it with your sisters, your sweetheart, or your close friends. Build in time for a rejuvenating lunch, leave the kids with a babysitter, and use the drive time to play your favorite music, listen to an audiobook, or, better still, catch up on each other's lives.

Remember that not all outlet malls are alike. Some have the predictable Carter's, OshKosh, Liz Claiborne, and Reebok outlets, while others, such as the Chelsea Premium Outlets chain, with locations from Orlando to Los Angeles and from Seattle to Boston, contain Barney's, Escada, Hugo Boss, BCBG Max Azria, Oilily, Burberry, and Ralph Lauren. Visit *www.premiumoutlets.com* and register your information so that you can enter the online "VIP Lounge" page, where you can print coupons and look for special events and savings.

If you can't afford to shell out the greenbacks required to purchase a new Fendi or Coach bag, you can still enjoy the pleasures of the clutch by visiting Bag Borrow or Steal, *www.bag-borroworsteal.com*. For a monthly fee ranging between $19.95 to $149.95, you can choose one of three main levels of membership (Trendsetter, Princess, or Diva), which will give you access to borrowing the latest brands and styles. The concept is similar to Netflix or Blockbuster's video-through-the-mail rental programs that allow you to check out videos and keep them as long as you like for a monthly fee, except this company loans you the hottest bags in town. When you are finished with them, pop them back in the mail to the company and choose more. If you fall in love with the bag you borrow, you can ask the company to let you buy it for a "steal." Membership includes a rental fee for one bag per month and a *What's in the Bag?* newsletter introducing all the latest handbag designers and trends for those who just can't let go of purse fashion.

Five-Star Fact

Think diamonds are a girl's best friend? Visit *www.jemzn jewels.com* for gently used jewelry from companies like Tiffany & Co. and designer watches from companies like Bedat.

If you're on a treasure hunt for designer clothes, consignment stores can offer tremendous finds. Generally, you'll want to visit the consignment stores in the wealthier areas of your town or even out of town. If you are vacationing in Vail, by all means find the gently used boutiques! If you are willing to sell some of your almost-new clothes at the store, you can use the credit toward your purchases. Most stores choose the sale price, then give you a percentage (typically 40 to 50 percent) if the item sells. Clothes taken in on consignment must be pressed, clean, and in good condition and can't be too out of style in most cases. Depending on the store, you may be able to land all kinds of designer clothes. If you can't find a consignment shop near your home, visit an online fashion resale store like *www.christabellescloset.com*. The site recently featured a pair of Prada Mary Janes for $80.

Vintage wear abounds at thrift stores such as Salvation Army and Goodwill. While the clothes may be used, you can almost always find a treasure on the rack or in the bins. Ask one of the employees or volunteers if there is a particular day when they restock the clothes aisles. You may even want to volunteer yourself. Watch for special promotions, such as discounts on certain days of the weeks, and visit regularly. Over time, you will stumble upon a few treasures. For example, we recently found a Kate Spade bag for $3. The same item was still listed on the Macy's website for $175!

Some of the best deals in town can be found in your sisters' or friends' closets. Do you have friends who wear similar size clothes or shoes? Spend a Saturday sorting through the unwanted and unworn and exchange them with a friend. Better yet, organize a Saturday event with women from your neighborhood. Invite women to exchange items for free or a small fee. If exchanging seems too difficult, why not hold a neighborhood garage sale? The profits can be spent on new items to go with your gently used finds or donated to the charity of your choice.

Another way to be fashionable without overspending is to combine your creative talents with those of friends and family. Add your own touches to plain jeans and jackets. If someone you know is an expert seamstress, ask her if she would be willing to trade out her fashion contributions to your wardrobe for something you can provide (babysitting, carpooling, typing services, etc.). If you are a wiz at the sewing machine, visit boutiques, websites, and magazines like *InStyle* or *People* to see the latest fashions you can re-create.

As for a lady's five-star wardrobe, you should definitely invest in the perfect "little black dress" that makes you feel good, flatters your figure, and goes just about anywhere. Pick out jeans with a good name and white pressed shirts for a classic casual outfit that never goes out of style, and find at least one to-die-for gown and pair of heels that make you feel like Cinderella every time you see them, just in case you are invited to the ball.

No matter what tags are tucked into the back of your

collar, you can add a star or two to your fashion lineup by remembering a few fashion basics:

- Add depth and interest to your outfit by mixing textures and fabrics.

- Buy clothes that naturally flatter your frame. Even inexpensive clothes look good if they have a tailored fit.

- Shop at your favorite expensive boutique or couture store on a quiet weekday. Explain to the salesperson that you are on a strict budget but want to learn about fashion. See if the clerk will take time to give you tips on what makes clothes stay in style and which colors and cuts flatter you most.

- Dress your age. Rejoice in each season of life and accept each stage gracefully by wearing the clothes that reflect where you are.

- Make sure your belt and shoes match. It's easy to mistake black for brown in a dimly lit room, but if you do everyone in the daylight will notice!

- If you want a slimmer look, incorporate scoop necks, V-necks, and darker colors. The general fashion rule of

Five-Star Fact

An increasing number of airports are sporting the latest from Gucci, Burberry, Cartier, and other Fifth Avenue-style boutiques in their duty-free area. So, what's the deal? If you are traveling abroad, you can save money on expensive perfume as well as designer clothes, makeup, and jewelry, but if you make a sizable purchase you need to calculate how much in taxes you are going to have to pay when you cross the U.S. border. You may be surprised to find that only a portion of your purchase is actually duty free and limits vary based on where you are traveling. It's also important to remember to note that duty free doesn't necessarily mean reduced price. Prices for the same item can vary widely based on which duty-free store you choose, and you may end up finding the same products at equal or lower prices online or in your own city.

★ ★ ★ ★ ★

thumb states that you should never pair a dark top with a lighter-colored bottom. Dark on the bottom, light on top.

- Unless you are pencil thin, horizontal stripes are a no-go.

- Dress up any outfit with a vintage brooch, big costume pearls, or chunky bracelets.

Beauty

Personal beauty products come in all sizes, shapes, scents, and price ranges. You can buy your product at specialty stores, department stores, or even mass merchandisers, and in the process pay anywhere from $1 to $150 or more for a single item.

The key is to find the look that is right for you—the one that makes you feel the most alive, the most put together, and the most attractive for the price you can afford. Schedule time for a makeover, usually offered at the cosmetic counters of any department store. If the cosmetic counter attendant is not busy, you may be able to walk right in. However, it is best to call ahead and book a makeover appointment. Each cosmetic line offers makeovers with their particular products, whether it is Estée Lauder, Clinique, Lancôme, Prescriptives, or an in-home presentation by a Mary Kay representative. The key is to find the combination of products that have the texture, scents, and colors that look and feel the best on you.

Be aware that the makeup artists at these counters have a

> ### Live It!
>
> Pay attention to the whole package you're presenting and make the best of what you have. Remove scuff marks from your shoes and remember to add accessories. Take good care of your nails and spend an extra minute on your makeup. Finally, don't forget a smile and the sparkle of joy in your eyes that tells everyone you meet that you are enjoying your five-star life!

wide variety of experience levels and personal preferences. Speak up if you feel makeup is being applied too heavily or in shades you would never wear, but also be open to their suggestions. If you love the look, you still do not have to buy every high-end product to re-create it. If it's important to you to get the exact same look, then go ahead and invest in the makeup line. But if the colors and application techniques are truly what have captured your eye, ask the clerk if she will guide you step-by-step through applying makeup yourself and buy a product or two from her. Then buy the rest elsewhere.

Give It!

Plan to buy at least one item from a beauty consultant who does a makeover and gives you makeup tips, as many work on a commission basis.

During your makeover, pay attention. Take notes on a small pad, if necessary, of the colors she recommends for you and why. Note where blush is applied, which colors of eyeshadow she uses, and how mascara can be applied on the top and underneath your lashes for a fuller look. Rather than buy everything on impulse, thank the clerk for her time, make a small purchase, and walk away from the cosmetic department for a while. Spend time in other parts of the store or mall and then duck into a restroom to see if the products she applied are holding up well. If you still like the look as much in different lighting, then decide whether to go back to the counter and purchase the whole package or try to choose the same colors in a different brand at a local drugstore or mass merchandiser.

If you choose to use the more expensive brands available at department stores, wait to buy until the company is having one of their "gift with purchase" or "purchase with purchase" offers that can give you more products for the same price. Estée Lauder, Lancôme, and Clinique are three companies that offer these types of promotions. Several times a year at different department stores, they will offer some kind of clutch or makeup bag filled with a lipstick or gloss, mascara, a sample-size skincare product, and either another makeup item, such as an eyeshadow or blush, or an accessory, such as a mirror or comb. The colors of the products and bags vary. All three companies will give these bags away with a certain dollar amount purchased (usually $20 to $30). Occasionally, a bag filled with many sample products will be offered as an additional purchase with a purchase. You can buy the bag of goodies for far less (usually under $30) than they would cost individually. The offers are one per customer, but clerks will often ring items separately if family members are all present and each want a bag. For example, my three teen girls and I will visit the Clinique counter to purchase foundation, skin-care products, powder, or eyeshadow. Each of us will have our item or items rung up separately (even though Mom is usually paying the whole bill), so that each of us receives a gift as long as our dollar amount meets the required minimum.

Look for seasonal offers, especially during the Christmas season. Estée Lauder comes out with an annual Blockbuster makeup kit that is a several-hundred-dollar value usually priced under $75 with a purchase of any fragrance item. The kits debut the day after Thanksgiving but can be preordered to ensure you don't miss out. When you are buying during the holidays, look for department store bonuses on top of the cosmetic counter offers, especially at Christmas time and during the Mother's and Father's Day seasons. At times, the stores will offer a crystal vase, a train case, a marble chess set, teddy bear, or other free gift when your purchases total a certain dollar amount throughout the cosmetic department or the store.

For example, last November I went into Macy's for a new powder from Clinique because the company was "in-gift" (the industry term for the time when gifts with your purchase are available). I noticed that the signs were up at the Estée Lauder counter advertising the upcoming annual

Blockbuster makeup kit. After finishing my purchase at Clinique (where the sales clerk was kind enough to give me lip gloss and fragrance samples for my teens, free for the asking with my purchase), I walked over to Estée Lauder to check out the kit. It was packaged in a useful train case, and the lipsticks and nail polishes were colors I would normally use. The clerk said I could preorder the kit and pointed out that there was also a coordinating bag promotion going right then, which she could set aside with my preorder. Additionally, the company was offering a beautiful plum shoulder tote filled with makeup products as a purchase with purchase that was the perfect gift for a relative, and there was also a free gift for purchasing that bag. As if that were not enough, Macy's was giving away free red train case luggage pieces with any cosmetics department purchase of $85 or more. So I spent $113 and ended up with more than $500 in high-end cosmetics and bags, with gifts galore for relatives and friends and the Blockbuster kit for me (to be given to me for Christmas by my husband, thereby helping him too!).

As a makeup fanatic, I don't limit myself only to department stores. Some of the biggest treasures come in inexpensive packages. Bonnie Bell lip gloss sticks that retail for just over a dollar are one of my favorite things in life, and I am thrilled to find great deals on Revlon, L'Oreal, Maybelline, Cover Girl, and other brands at my local Walgreens, CVS, Target, or Wal-Mart. Each of these companies has its own website and regularly offers special deals and promotions through the sites, newspaper ads, and store circulars. Revlon recently offered a sweetheart of a deal when it gave away thousands of red satin evening bags with any $10 Revlon purchase. But wait, there's more! Revlon upped the ante by giving away the red bag and two vouchers for free movie tickets if you spent just $15, and the bag and ticket vouchers—*plus* the popular romantic comedy DVD *Laws of*

Attraction, with Pierce Brosnan and Julianna Moore—were yours if you spent $20 on Revlon cosmetics.

Now, offers like these do require a little work on the part of the consumer. First, I found the offer by doing an online search for rebates and free items. When I found this offer, I registered on the Revlon site and printed out a rebate form for the free items. Then I headed to the store to do my shopping, choosing the drugstore whose current ad offered Revlon products on sale. And I pulled out my coupon pouch for an extra savings with my coupons. I chose to buy the full $20 worth of makeup, which I planned to use in my teen girls' Easter baskets. I mailed the receipt and my printed form filled out with the ten-digit UPC codes from each product to the company and waited the obligatory six to ten weeks for my goodies. The DVD retailed for around $20, as did the purse, and the movie ticket vouchers could be redeemed at virtually any movie theater around the country for up to a $12 ticket each. My freebies were worth $60, all for buying $20 of makeup.

Big cosmetic and health and beauty companies are very good at offering rebates, found in newspaper coupon sections, inside the products themselves, and in store rebate catalogs. Many will offer $10 back with $20 purchased or movie ticket vouchers when you spend a certain dollar amount. Combine the store specials and coupons with your manufacturer's coupons, mail in for a rebate, and you are shopping for many items virtually free.

One year, household brands giant Procter & Gamble offered a rebate I could not resist. For every $10 worth of P&G products you purchased, the company would send you a $20 gift certificate to the gourmet food and gifts company Harry & David. Talk about Five-Star Living! The certificates could be used in the exclusive Harry & David stores or online, and you could receive a total of five gift certificates per household. I bought $50 worth of laundry products, kitchen and bathroom cleaners, toothpaste, and other P&G products I use anyway and received $100 to spend at Harry & David. I chose to spend the certificates in the local Harry & David store and bought sparkling juices, cheesecakes, crackers, gourmet condiments, and candy, which I used at all my holiday parties. The store also offered a frequent buyer card and punched it for my purchases, entitling me to a free box of gourmet chocolate truffles!

If there are particular cosmetic or beauty products you just can't live without, search high and low for the best deals on them. In addition to paying full price at a department store, hundreds of thousands of top-brand cosmetics are available on the auction site eBay. If you have fallen in love with a $50 cream or makeup item or find that a particular product makes all the difference in your appearance, you can also price the items online at *www.froogle.com*, *www.shopping.com*, *www.pricegrabber.com,* and *www.bizrate.com* and land a better rate. A quick visit to sites such as *www.amazon.com* under beauty supplies can also produce a lower price.

> **Give It!**
>
> If you make use of coupons and rebates and find yourself inundated with toothpaste, deodorants, cleaning supplies, pet food, or other items you can't use, donate them to local animal shelters, homeless shelters, your church ministries, and other charities that can put them to good use.

At outlet malls, stores like the Cosmetics Company Store and Perfumania can be found. These outlets offer off-season brand-name items from all the big names, including the leftover "free gifts" which can be purchased for around $10 each. And speaking of fragrances, the same rule applies. Search for a new fragrance for yourself or your man around the holidays when fragrance companies beef up their offers by providing more gift sets and free gifts with purchase. Men's fragrances come with everything from beach towels or T-shirts to watches and remote-control cars, while ladies might receive a pretty tote, costume jewelry, a stuffed bear, or other fun item.

Another great way to keep yourself smelling fresh is to check out the bargains at Bath & Body Works and Victoria's Secret. Both stores are owned by the same company (which explains why some fragrances are very similar), and both offer affordable indulgences. If you don't mind adding another credit card, the Victoria's Secret credit card can be used in both stores and offers great free gifts each month for the first year that you have the card, with reward points and other special offers. Having the card also puts you on both stores' mailing lists. (Be aware that the Victoria's Secret catalogs will arrive regularly in your mailbox unless you ask the company not to send them.) Bath & Body Works is very good at regularly sending out coupons for free items with a purchase. The best part of having the credit card is that these stores accept credit payments in the store, so when I make a purchase, I have the clerk run my credit card through so that I can receive my points. When that transaction is finished, I simply write a check to pay for the purchase, and the clerk immediately applies it to my credit account. No monthly bill, and I still receive points and many offers for free items. In the last year, I have received and redeemed coupons for free candles, lip glosses, lotions, foot creams, body sprays, and aromatherapy products. Victoria's Secret even sends its credit customers a special gift (for the past few years it has been a $10 gift card—no purchase necessary) on their birthday.

Bath & Body Works' annual sale is one to watch, with fragranced soaps as low as $1 and holiday gift sets slashed as much as 75 percent. Both stores offer light fragrance sprays

Give It!

When you are expecting company who will stay in your home, place some of your health and beauty deals, makeup items, and luxury soaps into a pretty basket and place it in the room where they will stay. Your five-star treatment and amenities will make your guests feel pampered.

regularly at prices that are either six items for $30 to $35 or buy three, get one free. For just a few dollars, you can smell good—and so can your home—and that makes you feel good all over.

Hair and Nails

Our definition of Five-Star Living means that you do the very best with what you've got, so that you look and feel your best at the price that works for you.

With that in mind, you can choose a $10 haircut at the Supercuts down the street or the $200 one at the chic salon that has to be booked months ahead. The point is to spread your spending to achieve the most bang for the buck. If you love the way your hair is done at a particular salon and haven't seemed to be able to recreate the look anywhere else, pay for that cut and cut back in some other area.

If you enjoy having great nails, incorporate manicures and pedicures into your budget and revel in them. Maybe your body isn't quite in the shape you want it to be, or your clothes still need some work. But if your makeup, hair, or nails are just right, the way you feel will improve. It's all in the attitude, and we want you to absolutely exude confidence and joy. That's a five-star life!

If you prefer salon-brand hair products, Regis and Trade Secret are two chains of stores

Five-Star Fact

Has your all-time favorite lipstick been discontinued? Have no fear. It's Three Custom Color Specialists, *www.threecustom. com*, to the rescue! The New York City-based company has a list of the secret mixes of more than 7500 different lipstick colors and can recreate your favorite. You simply slip a small slice of your old color into a small bag and mail it to the company. For $50 they'll create two new tubes of your favorite color. The company can also recreate other types of makeup. It's pricey, but when it's your all-time favorite, it's worth it.

★ ★ ★ ★ ★

found in many malls that have great sales and rewards. At the Trade Secret in my area, the store offers an additional 20 percent off your entire purchase if you shop between 10 and 11 AM on Tuesdays. All day Tuesday the store also offers double punches on its reward card, and at Christmastime offers lots of gift sets, plus a cute teddy bear free with a $50 purchase. I shopped for hair care products for the whole family on a Tuesday morning in early December, chose better-value gift sets, received 20 percent off my purchase, got the teddy bear, and filled up my reward card with double punches, entitling me to $20 of free products. Check stores in your area for frequent buyer programs, reward cards, and special discounts.

Action Points

Beauty Bargains and Fashion Flair

★ Take advantage of all health and beauty rebates.

★ Decide which areas are the most important for you to invest in and which areas you can still look and feel good for less.

★ Look for brand-name bargains at thrift stores, consignment stores, and online.

★ Check out the brands you want from clothes to cosmetics on eBay.

★ Aim to buy cosmetics and fragrances around the holidays for better gift sets, promotions, and bonus items.

★ Aim for putting together the whole you, exuding confidence and joy inside and out.

★ Trade out your time and talents with friends who may be able to make over your denim, give you a makeover, trade clothes with you, or create masterpieces of fashion.

★ Every so often make shopping for something new an event. Enjoy friends or family, a great meal, and the time spent together as you shop.

Terrific Treats
for Tots to Tweens

Baby Dior, Versace Young, Rock Star Baby, elaborate birthday parties, and high-tech electronics. Today's kids have it all, or at least it seems as though we try to give it all to them. Our kids also have their own money, and they like to spend it. They love eating candy and ice cream and going to theme parks and to the movies. They want to decorate their rooms and own their own computers and cell phones.

Parents can quickly go overboard when they want their children to have it all—from custom-decorated bedrooms to the best birthday bashes in town. Without wise planning, Five-Star Living can quickly put a strain on a family's budget. Brand names and fun gadgets don't have to go by the wayside, but a wise shopper rarely walks to the full-price racks in the most elite boutiques and starts grabbing. Five-star shoppers look for the brands they want in other channels—from discount stores like Marshalls or T.J. Maxx to thrift stores, consignment shops, and even garage sales. They save money by using coupons on diapers, formula, and other necessities so that dollars are available for spending or giving in other areas.

Tiny Tots

Five-star savings are easy to find when you are expecting a little one or getting ready to adopt. Check around online or ask your doctor's office about free formula samples, magazine subscriptions, baby food offers, and more. Your obstetrician will most likely give you a diaper bag filled with freebies for infants, including photo studio coupons from stores such as Sears and JCPenney, formula samples, and other goodies. When you leave the hospital with your new baby, you should also receive sampler packs of many infant items.

Ongoing freebies for parents of the tiniest tots include free six-month subscriptions to *American Baby* magazine, a *Better Homes & Gardens* publication that can be found at *www.americanbaby.com*, and *Baby Talk* magazine, a *Parenting* magazine publication found at *www.parenting.com*.

Beech-Nut, Gerber, Heinz, and other baby food makers rely on coupons to keep customers coming back, as do the makers of baby formula like Similac, Enfamil, and Carnation Good Start. If you sign up online, at the doctor's office, or through the mail for their money-saving offers, you will receive coupons, samples, and dated money-saving "checks" (made out to the retailer, not to you) that operate like coupons.

For baby's entertainment, there are a variety of mail-order book and toy clubs that send free items, plus an additional product to "preview." The free items truly are free, but the catch is that you must be organized and responsible enough to send the preview item back on time (and sometimes at your own expense) and cancel your subscription during the trial period, or you will be obligated to pay for the previewed item and will receive new toys or books to preview every three to six weeks. You must buy the products or keep shipping them back until you cancel your subscription.

From bibs to child safety products, there are many other freebies for babies. Most offers can be found online, but be choosy with which offers you give your full contact information. Be sure to read the "terms of agreement" every time and give your address, e-mail address, and phone number only to companies you know are legitimate. If you sign up for every freebie offer on the Net, your e-mail inbox will not be able to hold all the promotional e-mails you will begin receiving.

One special offer for babies is a free ticket to the Ringling Bros. Barnum & Bailey Circus to be redeemed anytime during their lifetime. Parents must sign up for the Baby's First Circus voucher online at *www.ringling.com* when their child is under one year old. The voucher is sent through the mail and can be redeemed for one ticket to any Ringling Bros. circus. Although the offer makes it clear that there is a maximum of one voucher per household per year and that you must sign up to receive the voucher before your child's first birthday, the company has made provisions for multiple births and adoptions of children over one year. Once you sign up, Ringling uses your contact information to notify your family each year when the circus is headed your way by sending coupons or other special ticket offers.

> ### Give It!
> If your outgrown designer-brand kids clothes are still in great shape, put the Live It! Give It! principles to work and give them to a struggling single parent, a local pregnancy center, or sell them on eBay or at a garage sale and give a portion of the proceeds away.

Five-Star Living parents can be prudent while keeping their baby decked out in style by leaving the tags on all new infant clothing (that you purchased or received as a gift) until you are ready to use it and tucking the receipts into an envelope or other safe place. Because babies grow at different rates, the chances are very good that you will have more than a few new clothing items that can't be worn because they are too big, too small, or the wrong season. You can easily return unworn items with the tags if they were purchased within the last 90 days, and many stores honor returns for an even longer period. For gifts, get to know the brand names sold by each store so that you can return items to the right place for store credit. If items cannot be returned, or you would rather bless someone with them, consider the Live It! Give It! principles and donate them to someone in need, to your local crisis pregnancy or women's resource center, or to your local homeless shelter. The fair market value of the donation can be listed on your federal income taxes if you itemize your deductions. Intuit's ItsDeductible and H&R Block's Deduction Pro software run about $20 each (and are often free with rebate if you purchase a full tax program), and they calculate the value of every item you have donated. Remember to get a receipt from the charity when you drop off your goods and to write a general list on it of what you gave.

Designer baby clothes are just so cute you could buy them by the barrelful. However, parents should use restraint when choosing the toniest wardrobe for their little princes and princesses. To see what brands are at the top of the list, visit online company Tutti Bella's running blog *www.whatshotfortots.blogspot.com* for brand descriptions and online boutiques.

If you want to get a hands-on education of what brands to

> ### *Fun Fact*
>
> Many babies of celebs have *interesting* names. Consider the monikers these kids carry: Apple (daughter of Gwyneth Paltrow and singer Chris Martin of the rock band Coldplay); Phinnaeus and Hazel (the twins of Julia Roberts and photographer Danny Moder); Coco (daughter of actors Courteney Cox and David Arquette); Scout, Rumer, and Tallulah (daughters of actors Demi Moore and Bruce Willis), and Peaches Honeyblossom, Pixie, and FiFi Trixibelle (daughters of musician Bob Geldof and the late Paula Yates).

buy, browse the chicest boutiques in your area and wherever you vacation. You can learn the brands without buying and take note of how items are grouped together on displays to learn the art of accessorizing. Take your newfound knowledge of Versace Young, Shescrafty heirloom handknits, and Burberry and apply it when browsing through eBay, a discount store, garage sales, or thrift stores. For the small fry, finding excellent quality gently used clothing is a cinch. Everyone likes their baby to look the best, so designer clothes that have been worn only a time or two abound at children's consignment stores and the like.

Five-Star Fact

Rock 'n' roll star Tico Torres of the popular band Bon Jovi helped develop a trendy brand of infant onesies, T-shirts, and sleepers called Rock Star Baby. Check out *www.rockstarbaby.de* for the latest styles.

★ ★ ★ ★ ★

The same methods can be used when it comes to designing baby's room. Visit high-end children's furniture and bedroom stores and look at the items grouped together. See what features different brands include, and learn the brands and manufacturers. That way, if you run into the same furniture at a much lower price, you will know exactly what you are getting. If you are afraid to paint the walls of the nursery yourself, ask friends for recommendations of a local artist, even a top high school or college student, who would custom design a mural or look for your nursery at a fraction of professional prices.

Live It!

If you love designer brands for your baby, look for them at thrift stores, consignment shops, garage sales, and on eBay. You can still have the brands but at a fraction of the price.

Celebrity nursery decorator Wendy Bellissimo suggests picking the fabrics you want for your kids' rooms first, then getting flat, scrubbable paint that complements your fabrics and theme. High-gloss enamel paints can make an infant's room too bright. She also suggests hardwood

Live It!

When buying baby furniture, consider how you want to use it. You can choose a traditional crib and changing table you can pass along or donate after your baby is too old for it or choose a crib that converts into a regular bed and a short dresser with a removable changing table top or pad.

floors rather than carpet because they are easier to clean and keep dust free.

Junior Deals and Steals

Even big families can experience Five-Star Living without breaking the bank or forgetting all the fun. While cross-country trips to Walt Disney World may not be in the budget every year, there are plenty of opportunities for five-star fun all around. Even in your hometown.

One way to make memories is to check around for report card rewards in your area. Many local businesses and national chains offer rewards for good grades. The national chain of hip girls' clothing Limited Too offers $5 in free merchandise each quarter for passing grades (they don't even have to be As!). The $5 can be spent on anything in the store without obligation to purchase anything else. Even my sons like to "cash in" on this deal because Limited Too has candy priced under $5. They walk out with a free treat and the incentive to keep studying hard.

Many video rental stores offer a free movie rental for good grades, and some local arcades as well as Chuck E. Cheese and Celebration Station offer free tokens for

Five-Star Fact

You can introduce your kids to your favorite treats of the past by offering them some BB Bats, MoonPies, SweetTarts, Dots, wax bottles, or striped candy sticks. Grab some at Cracker Barrel or visit *www.eBulkCandy. com* and *www.sweetnostalgia. com*, where you can find everything from Zotz to Necco Wafers. *EBulkCandy.com* even offers three-pound assortments of "decade" candy for less than $30. You can choose from pre-1950s, 1950s, 1960s, or 1970s.

★ ★ ★ ★ ★

As, Bs, and Cs (with a limit of 10 or 15 per quarter). Some Krispy Kreme donut stores offer one free donut per A (up to six As), and you can check with other local businesses for report card reward offers. Keep report cards (or a copy of them if you have to return yours to your school) in your glove compartment with your coupons or in a portable organizer so you always have them with you.

Reading is a wonderful Five-Star Living pastime with great payoffs for everyone. Create family night opportunities that include curling up with a good book and taking turns reading aloud. Or pick up dramatic audio versions of classic books and listen together as a family. Good books entertain all ages, reinforce reading and listening skills, increase vocabulary, and provide family time together in an intimate setting that is relaxing and stress free. Visit bookstores to get little ones looking forward to reading on their own, and always offer plenty of books for older kids to read.

Another five-star family fun time can be found at local libraries. Has it been years since you visited one? Did you know that libraries have come a long way? Not only are they great places for borrowing books, but also libraries now have music CDs, books on tape and CD, DVDs and VHS copies of popular movies (thereby saving you those rental fees), and free Internet access. Libraries are wonderful places to find out about educational presentations, local author talks and signings, and other community events. You can even request that your library obtain specific materials you would like to see on the shelves. Of course, the library can't always order everything you want, but book buyers like to receive input and often do not get it. If you ask for something, it may come.

Stores also like to encourage kids to read, and summertime is a great time to look for special rewards for reading. National chains like Barnes & Noble and Borders usually do some type of summer reading club, with prizes, books, or other small treats for reading certain books or a certain

Live It!

One five-star family night that won't cost you a fortune could be visiting your local bookstore during a time when they offer live entertainment in the café, story hour in the kids' section, or other family-oriented activities. During special events, ask the store if they offer additional discounts or incentives for making a purchase.

number of books. Local bookstores and some Christian bookstores have their own reading programs and book clubs that offer fun for the whole family.

Pizza Hut sponsors the Book It! program, where teachers can give monthly coupons for free individual one-topping pizzas to each student who achieves the set reading goal for the month. Homeschool teachers are also eligible to participate in this program and receive pizza coupons for their children. Visit *www.bookitprogram.com* for more information.

When kids are out of school for the summer, inexpensive entertainment options abound. Many movie theater chains offer free or reduced-price family-friendly movies at least once a week, usually in the mornings. The theater hopes you will spend money on concessions, but that is not required. Teach your children that just seeing the movie is a treat in itself, or for five-star bonus points take them for a special snack before or after the show.

It's Your Birthday

Kids under the age of 12 can find a wealth of birthday offers from a variety of retailers. Some party store chains offer free balloons, while ice cream and fast-food chains from Blimpie to Marble Slab offer free sandwiches, meals, or ice-cream cone certificates via snail mail or e-mail to the birthday boy or girl. Participating businesses have included Bob Evans, ACE hardware stores, Denny's, Captain D's, Burger King, and California Pizza Kitchen. Once these offers come in, keep them in your glove compartment, coupon pouch, or organizer in the car so that you never have to hunt them down or regret that you don't have them with you.

In addition to birthday freebies, birthday parties are always a big deal as they entail deciding where to have them, how many children to invite, what food to serve, and what kind of entertainment to have. Five-star birthdays can be organized without spending a fortune if you put your time and talents to work. First, ask your children what themes and activities they would enjoy. Give them options that will work within your spending limit, from having just a couple of select friends join them at a specific restaurant to inviting a larger group to a local park, beach, or your backyard. If you live near a theme park that your child loves to visit, it may be more economical to take one parent, the birthday child, and one friend to the theme park for the day than to have a birthday party.

When planning a party, consider all the costs. Decorations, cake, candles, party food and drinks, activities, game materials, the location rental, equipment rental, entertainers, balloons, and goodie bags must all be taken into consideration. Once you know how much you can spend and your child's chosen theme, set about the tasks you can accomplish on your own and decide how you will organize the rest. For example, if you are having a birthday party in your yard, make a contingency plan for bad weather. Make sure you have enough chairs and food for the parents who might stay or enough adult supervision in case parents do not stay.

Decide whether to make a fancy birthday dessert, buy one, or enlist a friend's help. If your friend is artistic and you are organized, perhaps you can trade off duties for the parties you must each coordinate. Your friend might be willing to make the cake, special decorations, or be in charge of an arts and crafts activity, and you can return the favor for her parties by making sure items get ordered, invitations go out, and the events stay on schedule.

For girls, sleepovers are usually a big hit. Keep the group of girls small, and try to have an even number so that no one feels left out. You can build a movie night theme, a "dance" party with lots of music, a makeover party (where you bring in a Mary Kay or home beauty consultant to show the girls how to clean their faces properly or put on makeup), a "spa" party with manicures or pedicures, or a pool party.

For boys, anything that centers around video games or an outdoor activity is likely to be a success. Allow them to race skateboards and scooters (with proper supervision), hit and throw balls, play "manhunt," or head for the skating rink. One idea we found on the Internet is to hire a physical fitness instructor to engage the kids in activities that will send them home flat worn-out. (The kids will have a ball, and you'll be their parents' new best friend.)

For an extra special treat, hire a magician, a clown, a bouncy moonwalk, or a trained animal, such as a pony, to entertain the young audience. Better yet, ask around to find a friend or family member who will volunteer their services in this department.

For great cakes, ideas abound on the Internet, and each month *Family Fun* magazine offers illustrated step-by-step instructions for fantastic cakes from dinosaurs to mermaids. This magazine is also a wealth of resources for family activities, party planning, and easy arts and crafts. Another awesome site for party ideas and step-by-step directions is *www.coolest-kid-birthday-parties.com*, which includes both pictures and

Live It!

Tween girls love decorating their rooms, so one fun idea is to let the sleepover friends build "rooms" of their own. Gather enough shoeboxes so that each guest has one, then provide stickers, buttons, glue, sequins, tissue and wrapping paper, pipe cleaners, and other craft materials of all kinds and let the girls create miniature furniture and works of art for their shoebox "room." Two great books on making miniatures are *Tiny Treasures: Amazing Miniatures You Can Make!* (American Girl Library, $9.95) and *Micro Minis: Create Teeny Tiny Rooms with Your Own Style and Flair* (American Girl Library, $17.95). *Micro Minis* even comes with the supplies to build a tiny living room and bedroom.

directions for Hummer cakes, pirate cakes, Barbie cakes, and just about any other kind of cakes, as well as theme ideas, decorations, activities, and printable invitations.

Kids' Meals

Eating out can be expensive for families, but there are plenty of ways to enjoy fine dining or fast food and still keep your spending within reason. Many restaurants offer "kids eat free" programs all the time or on certain nights of the week. Some offer unlimited kids' meals with only one adult meal purchased. Some limit their offer to one free kids' meal per paid adult. For a listing of some of the deals in your area, check out *www.kidseatfree.com* and click on your state or the state you'll be visiting for a list of restaurant names, program details, and contact information. Always contact the restaurant to make sure the program is still in effect before counting on it.

Money Management for Kids

Children need to be taught at a young age how to handle and spend money wisely. Even preschool children age three or four can begin lessons in how to save, give, and spend with very small allowances. Studies show that today's children often have more disposable income than their parents, and it's never too soon to start teaching ways to make the most of it. Begin teaching your kids the Live It! Give It! principles now, so that they will grow up managing money, time, and talents well.

Give school-age children (or younger, if the children are ready) a weekly allowance and a check register to keep track of their spending. Help them deduct at least ten percent for giving and allow your kids to help decide where their "giving money" should be spent. They will be more excited about giving if they get to choose.

Also encourage your kids to put ten percent in savings

Live It!

Reward your children for putting more than the minimum required into their long-term savings by matching whatever extra they put away. For example, if your daughter receives $10 weekly and is required to save $1 of it but chooses to give you $2, match the extra dollar for a total of $3 going into her savings that week.

each week, allowing them to spend the rest. Each week at allowance time, ask your kids to show that their registers balance by producing the register and any money they have left. This will show you (and them) where their money is going. If they can't find their register, they lose their allowance for the week. If the register does not balance, deduct any missing amount or overage from the new allowance. Once your kids lose their money, they'll quickly get the hang of keeping track of it!

As they begin learning where their money is actually going, show them how to compare prices, clip coupons, receive rebates, and balance a budget. One preteen who used the check register method discovered after a few weeks that most of her weekly allowance was spent on individual bottles of soda she purchased at convenience stores for $1.19 each. Once she realized this, she chose to step up to Five-Star Living by spending $2.50 for a six-pack of the same soda at the grocery store. She consumed the same amount of soda, but she had more than $4 left over to buy something else.

When your children have money to spend, try to let them make their own choices on how to spend it, and then let them feel the consequences when they make a mistake. They may choose to go to the dollar store and buy toys that quickly fall apart. After a few times, gently point out that these toys are not built to last. You can then teach your child some of the differences between quality (buying a $10 toy that is built of sturdier materials) and quantity (buying ten of a similar but poorly constructed toy). Some children will decide to wait and spend more money on the better-quality toy; however, some will still want to go to the dollar store. If the thrill for your child is in the hunt, ten trips to the store will seem better than one, no matter what he takes home and how long it lasts. By teaching these beginning Live It! Give It! principles, you will gain insight into your child's personality and methods of problem solving, as well as set your child on the road to Five-Star Living.

Terrific Treats for Tots to Tweens

★ Become brand educated by visiting upscale boutiques and furniture stores.

★ Check for the brands you want at consignment stores, thrift stores, and garage sales.

★ Look for report card rewards at local retailers, and let your kids enjoy the free fruits of their hard work.

★ Trade out birthday party organization and execution with friends.

★ Find fun outings that utilize local resources and save you time and money (parks, libraries, beaches, and more).

★ Discover the joy in reading together as a five-star family. The benefits are priceless.

★ Teach your children the importance of saving and giving.

★ Allow kids to have some control over their own spending, saving, and giving decisions.

★ Show children the difference between quantity and quality.

Gourmet Groceries and Decadent Dining

Have you ever read those magazine articles where the women describe how they walked into the grocery store with a cart and three kids and walked out with $95 worth of grocery items that they paid nothing for, plus $10 in their pocket that they did not have when they walked in? (And, no, they did not sell one of the kids.) It all seems more than a little unrealistic, doesn't it? Coupons and rebates can seem like a lot of work. And you have to wonder if you're really buying anything you would really use anyway.

While $95 of free stuff and extra cash in your pocket is an extreme case of wheeling and dealing and not something the average person can pull off every day, coupons and rebate programs can be more valuable and much less difficult than they appear, saving you an average of $10 to $20 for every $100 spent on food items, cleaning supplies, health and beauty items, and paper and plastic goods. Additionally, when the items you buy with coupons or rebates are also on sale, your savings can double or triple. With rebates, some items do become free or you may even come out slightly ahead.

How do five-star shoppers do it? With knowledge, organization, and the right tools on hand.

The quickest way to cut your food budget and preserve your health is to cook at home rather than eat out. Not only will you save money, but also you can save time and calories with a little extra planning.

Live It!

Many store discount cards can be registered at UPromise, a website that offers "rebates" for shopping at participating stores and online retailers. The rebates are put into an online account for your kids to use for college. For more information, visit *www.upromise.com*.

If your store offers a value card, signing up will give you access to special prices, sales, and coupons. Be aware that you are trading your contact information and spending habits for the discounts. Grocery stores use your membership information to track your purchases and buying patterns, occasionally targeting you with specific offers. You will lose some of your privacy, but you will find a lower price on the groceries you buy.

To take advantage of specials and coupon savings, subscribe to your local paper at least on Sundays or buy it each week. If you don't mind the drive to the newspaper office each Monday morning, many newspapers will give you leftover coupon inserts. Go through the manufacturer's coupon sections faithfully, cutting out only the ones for products you regularly use or would like to try. Put them in your organizer or file, and don't forget to keep them in your car.

Scan the grocery store ads weekly as soon after they come out as you can. Circle the items you know you need or will use, and look through your coupons to see what additional money you can save on those items. Pull out those coupons and keep them in a bag with the ad, or place an asterisk inside the item circled on the ad so that you remember to use these manufacturer's coupons when you get to the store. Don't forget to use the store coupons within the ads as well (many of which can be combined with the manufacturer's coupons), and check *www.coolsavings.com*, *www.valupage.com*, or *www.coupons.smartsource.com* for immediately printable coupons before you go.

Keep rebate forms with the coupons you are using and determine if the items you are required to buy are items you need anyway. If they are on sale or a good price, buy them in order to receive the rebate. Check the rebate requirements carefully, such as the expiration date and what must be mailed in with the form. If the rebate requires an original receipt and you need your receipt in case other items must be returned or if you have multiple rebates, have your rebate items rung up separately so as to have receipts you can mail in. If the rebate requires that a UPC code be mailed also, cut the codes off of packages as soon as you get home and immediately place them in an envelope or ziplock bag with the receipt.

One recent example of a good rebate was $10 cash back offered with the purchase of three 12-pack cans of Pepsi products and three large bags of Frito-Lay chips. At local CVS stores, the soda went on sale with the stores' discount card for three 12-packs for $9, while chips were on sale for $2 per bag. The price of the items was then $15, minus $2 in manufacturers' coupons, for a total of $13 plus tax. Ten dollars was returned via the rebate, so the total cost for the 36 cans of soda and three large bags of chips (a retail value before the sale prices of around $22) was $3.21, plus a 37-cent stamp, an envelope, and the few minutes required to fill out

> **Give It!**
>
> Take advantage of coupon and rebate offers for products you don't buy and give the items away. For example, even if you don't have an animal, you can buy dog or cat food on sale and combine it with coupons so it costs next to nothing. Then, donate the supplies to your local animal shelter.

the form, clip UPC codes, address the envelope, and drop it in the mail.

Rebate forms for a variety of items can be found in the weekly coupon circulars, inside products, or online. Keep the ones you are likely to use and be sure to follow all directions. Some rebates offer a refund of an item's full price just for trying it. This works great if the product was several dollars, but might not be worth it if the retail was less than a buck (and you had to spend time, an envelope, and a stamp for the rebate).

Other grocery store savings can be found by watching for double or triple coupon promotions, where stores will double the face value of any coupon (usually one per item and up to 50¢). This adds up to a considerable savings. Some grocery store chains offer senior discounts, discounts once a week for being a AAA member (Winn Dixie stores offer an additional five percent off your entire purchase on Mondays if you are a AAA member), and extra coupons that print at the register. Watch your weekly flyers for special promotions too, such as free items or additional money off your entire bill when you spend certain amounts within a specific time period.

As you travel down the aisles, there are other savings tips to keep in mind. When buying meat, five-star shoppers enjoy fresh meat when it's on sale, but also learn which cuts preserve well when frozen. Here are a few shopping tips to keep in mind:

- Evaluate the entire package of meat for its fat and gristle content before buying. Look for leaner cuts.

- Ask the butcher to grind up a London broil steak when it's on sale for use as low-fat premium ground meat.

- Pork shoulder roasts can become shoulder blade steaks if you ask the butcher to slice it for you.

- Inexpensive cuts of beef, such as chuck steak, can be cut into thin pieces and used in fajitas and soups.

- Leftover pork, chicken, and beef can be used in soups, salads, and sandwiches.

- Fall is usually a good time to buy chicken, as stores tend to have more sales on chicken during this time of year.

When buying fruits and vegetables, here are a few things to remember:

Live It!

Looking for a healthy, easy, inexpensive breakfast? Make fresh fruit smoothies. Take a banana, peach, mango, berries—you pick your favorites—and throw them in a blender with some soy milk, fruit nectar, and ice. Blend it all together (add a small amount of honey if it is too tart for your taste) and enjoy! Freeze any leftovers for later.

- Make friends with the staff at your local grocery store. Find out the days fresh fruits and vegetables are delivered and put on sale. Plan to shop on those days, if you can.

- Fruits and vegetables are the most plentiful during the spring, summer, and fall. If you're looking for fresh goodies during the winter months, look for more affordable staples such as apples, oranges, bananas, lettuce, and carrots. Citrus ripens in the winter and should be the least expensive then.

- If you get a chance to shop at a farmer's market or produce stands, take advantage of the opportunity. You'll not only be helping out the local economy, but also you will save a bundle on the freshest goods around—many of which are organic. Don't forget your checkbook or cash since most local vendors don't take plastic.

Live It!

For a special treat, allow your kids to visit the bakery of the grocery store if they have been well behaved. Many stores offer a free cookie to each child, and some give out helium-filled balloons or other goodies.

- A big five-star pleasure is growing your own fruits or vegetables. You don't have to start a farm, but consider planting tomatoes or spices such as basil, oregano, parsley, or thyme. Your efforts will be rewarded in your delicious home-cooked meal.

When buying general grocery items, you may want to consider:

- You deserve a five-star meal. Skip prepackaged whenever you can. Instead, cook from scratch. Not only will your meals taste better, but also they will be more nutritious.

- In order to be able to cook from scratch, save time by cooking and prepping your food days before. For example, use Sunday evenings to cook all the bacon you will need for the week, boil eggs, grill meats, or cut up fruits and veggies.

- Decide on your menus a week or month ahead of time and list all the ingredients you will need before you head to the store. Buy everything you can that will last, and then make quick trips every few days for perishable items.

- If at all possible, leave the kids at home. You'll find yourself coming home with the products you need without all the extras and without all the frustration.

- If the kids are with you, give them each a limit on what they may ask for or contribute to the cart. Allow them $5 to spend or two items each which will help satisfy their desire to load up on goodies.

- Don't shop hungry. This is a simple rule but so easy to forget. Grab a protein bar or an apple before you begin shopping, and drink a glass or bottle of water. You'll be far less likely to overbuy.

- Buying in bulk can save you money, but not if you can't use the full amount before it expires.

- Generic brands often offer the lowest initial price, but be careful to check out the quality and flavor. Do not sacrifice taste or freshness for a lower price. You will not be satisfied and will be better off with name-brand items.

- Shopping multiple stores may not save you as much money as you think—especially when you calculate the time and gas used to drive to each location. Look for stores that match competitors' prices and carry all the ads in your car each week.

- See if any stores in your area double or triple coupon values. This will double or triple your savings.

Give It!

When you are at the grocery store, pick up an extra bag or two of items to give away. Drop them off with a neighbor in need (leaving them anonymously on the front porch or doorstep is the most fun!) or take them to a food pantry. While you are there, consider asking them how you could help further—by collecting donations, handing them out, praying for the ministry, or bringing food regularly.

Now, just because you cook your own food doesn't mean it can't be five-star delicious. Small upgrades to recipes you already know and enjoy can add flavor and a fresh spin on your meals. If you're making a grilled cheese sandwich, why not use Gouda or Brie instead of a basic American or cheddar? By upgrading the bread or adding a little prosciutto, you can spice up a basic sandwich into something that's gourmet.

Two-Star vs. Five-Star Foods

Looking to upgrade a meal? Here are some basic upgrades for common foods:

Cheese:	Cheddar	Brie
Bread:	White/whole wheat	Artisan stone-baked bread, sourdough
Meat:	Bologna/ham	Prosciutto

Nuts:	Peanuts	Roasted almonds, macadamia nuts
Veggies:	Celery/carrots	Artichoke hearts
Lettuce:	Iceberg	Spring mix or baby spinach
Dressing:	Ranch	Caesar, balsamic vinaigrette
Olives:	Black	Calamata, green picholine
Mushrooms:	White	Portobello, chanterelle

One thing to be aware of when you grocery shop is that stores are designed to encourage impulse buying. The entire layout of your local store has been assessed and reassessed to maximize sales. That is why all the endcaps (ends of the aisles) are loaded with irresistible treats at unbelievable prices. You are not supposed to go home without purchasing those products. In fact, some companies are even willing to pay the grocery stores for product placement at the end of aisles.

The best way to combat the tendency to overshop is simply by making a list of the products you need before you ever walk in the store. If you enjoy shopping sales (which we highly recommend), then pick up a newspaper with the local grocery inserts while you are still at home. Compare prices between the stores and make your shopping list based on the products you actually need. Once you are in the store, stick to the list unless you stumble upon an incredible deal you know you'll use.

When it comes to gourmet groceries, sales at local grocery stores can help you save money on general gourmet grocery items. Fresh markets and special delivery services can also help. In addition, Trader Joe's, *www.traderjoes.com*, offers good prices and occasional great discounts on an assortment of gourmet goodies. You will find all kinds of hard-to-find sweets and treats as well as coffees, teas, gourmet pastas, sauces, and other food items. You can also find deals on all kinds of gourmet treats online by doing a quick search on *www.froogle.com*. Another great site to visit is *www.epi cureanfoods.com* which offers a wide range of gourmet goods—many at a reduced price.

Recipes

Before you buy another cookbook, you need to go online and review some of the thousands of free recipes available from reputable sources. If you don't recognize the recipe's source, compare the ingredients to other online recipes for the same item online to make sure it's accurate. Several sites offer to deliver recipes via e-mail. Subscriptions are free at sites such as *www.daily message.com/recipe.shtml* and the Food Network, *www.food network.com*.

Magazine subscriptions are another low-cost, fun way to expand your recipe collection. Publications including *Cooking Light, Gourmet, Bon Appetit, Food and Wine,* and *Fine Cooking* deliver new recipes right to your door.

Cookbooks are available from a variety of famous chefs such as Emeril Lagasse, the Barefoot Contessa, the Naked Chef, and the Iron Chefs, among others. If you just have to have the taste of restaurant fare, check out Todd Wilbur's *Top Secret Restaurant Recipes: Creating Kitchen Clones from America's Favorite Restaurant Chains* (Plume Books, $14). In fact, Wilbur has an entire

Five-Star Fact

Godiva Chocolate is not only known for its superior quality and taste, but also for its full retail price. While an occasional box of Godiva will be featured on sale at Costco or other mass retail stores around the holidays, the best deals on Godiva are found online. The chocolatier is known for its holiday spin on its sweets and colorful box designs, so shortly after Christmas or Valentine's Day you can score a box of your own at the company's website for a deliciously reduced price.

Five-Star Fact

If you have ever wanted to enjoy the meals of the rich and famous, then you can do so for a fraction of the cost by buying a cookbook penned by the chef. For example, if you ever wanted to dine at the White House but still haven't received an invitation, then you might want to consider the cookbook *Dessert University* (Simon & Schuster, $40). The book, written by Roland Mesnier, who served as the pastry chef for the White House for more than 25 years, includes more than 300 of his executive treats. Endorsed by five First Ladies, the book features mouthwatering delicacies any sweet tooth will enjoy.

★ ★ ★ ★ ★

series of books that offer do-it-yourself recipes on favorite foods such as International House of Pancake's Cheese Blintzes, Hard Rock Cafe's Famous Baby Rock Watermelon Ribs, Cinnabon Cinnamon Rolls, and Little Caesar's Crazy Bread. Whether you're craving Denny's, Shoney's, the Cheesecake Factory, Pizza Hut, or another popular restaurant chain, within this book you'll discover how to clone some of their best meals. You can also find recipes for many restaurant favorites online at *www.copykat.com* and *www.topsecretrecipes.com*. On these sites, you can find recipes for Olive Garden Stuffed Mushrooms and Planet Hollywood's Potstickers, plus hundreds more.

Dining Out

If groceries are great but you really enjoy a nice meal out, or even a fast-food meal as long as you are not doing the cooking and cleaning, you're not alone! According to AARP, 44 percent of all adults eat in a restaurant in a given day. While the majority of those meals are fast food, a good portion of them are individuals and families enjoying sit-down meals. Five-star diners take full advantage of the multiple coupons, discounts, and free food programs available at thousands of restaurants around the country. From Entertainment Books to fund-raising discount cards to newspaper coupons, good deals are everywhere when it comes to food. Bon appetit!

Finding Fast Food

Fast-food coupons abound for the savvy shopper. While newspapers and mail stuffers (aka junk mail) are prime hunting grounds for the 2-for-1 sandwich offer, some of the best coupons appear on the back of receipts from some local grocery stores. Amid ads and offers for discount oil changes and dance lessons, you'll find easy-to-clip coupons for a variety of fast-food chains. Simply hold on to that portion of the receipt and enjoy extra savings the next time you need a quick burger and fries. Look in local stores and shops for free coupon booklets that contain fast-food offers, and take a look at local school fund-raiser cards that students sell. A $10 investment can get you free pizza, buy-one-get-one (known as BOGO offers) sub sandwiches, or free French fries and drinks.

Look for annual coupon calendars to be sold at Christmastime from popular fast food chains like Chick-Fil-A and Subway. Each month, the calendar contains a coupon for a free or free-with-purchase item. Most calendars retail for around $5, and some are discounted after the holiday. Chick-Fil-A calendars are a real win-win at their $5 price, as they are packed with more than $30 in coupons for free food (from free Chick-Fil-A sandwiches to ice-cream cones), and the company allows schools and churches to sell the calendars at a profit as fund-raisers. This company supports many local organizations, offers educational toys from some of

Give It!

For true five-star cooking, preserve your family's history and your favorite memories by creating a personalized family cookbook. Morris Press Cookbooks, *www.morriscookbooks. com*, allows each family member to go online and input recipes. The company then assembles the recipes into a softcover, hardback, or three-ring cookbook, complete with dividers, pictures, even family history, depending on which package you choose, for under $5 each. Our family cookbook features a family photo from 1890, several pages of family history, a table of contents, and hundreds of recipes—each listing the contributor's name and their branch of the family tree. The hardback books cost about $4 each and were sold to family members for $10 each, with the profits going into a special scholarship fund that will be donated in our family's name to local students.

the top children's companies in its Kids Meals, and is closed on Sundays so its employees can have time for their families and faith. Chick-Fil-A makes it a point to practice the Live It! Give It! principles and is our choice for the best Five-Star Living fast-food chain.

In some areas, McDonald's, Wendy's, and other fast-food outlets sell booklets of ten coupons for $1, redeemable for free small fries, cookies, a junior drink, or an ice-cream cone. The booklets appear around Halloween (to be used as Halloween treats) and sometimes Valentine's Day, and they are great to have on hand. Krispy Kreme and Domino's have great fund-raiser cards profitable for buyers and sellers. If you have an organization that needs to raise money, Krispy Kreme cards are $5 each and can be sold for $10. Each card entitles the bearer to buy a dozen donuts and get one free—up to 10 or 12 times. The Domino's fund-raiser cards can be purchased by a nonprofit organization for $3 and sold for $10. Each card gives the buyer 12 free items from Domino's, including one small, one medium, and one large one-topping pizzas, plus cinnamon breadsticks, buffalo wings, and other items. One item can be redeemed per visit, and no purchase is necessary. For $10, the bearer receives more than $65 worth of food.

If you're trying to make the most of your fast-food experience, it's important to remember that location plays an enormous role in the pricing of food. A McDonald's value meal in a small town in Kansas is likely to be several dollars less than one at a ski resort in Colorado. Prices can vary even within the same cities and towns, so if you're counting every dollar, it may pay to shop around.

Moderate and Fine Food

When it comes to fine food establishments, promotions can be more difficult to find, but they are out there. Be sure to explore every offer you can find. If there's a new restaurant opening in your area, take advantage of their grand opening deals and discounts. Find out how long the promotion will last, and if you enjoyed your visit, then book another reservation.

Always let a restaurant know if you're celebrating a special occasion—both at the time you make the reservation and discreetly when you arrive. You may be entitled to a free beverage or dessert, but more importantly, you will be guaranteed extra attention from the servers.

Many moderately priced restaurants and some fine dining establishments offer early bird or sunset menus with reduced prices. In the past, chains such as Olive Garden have allowed guests to order a lunch-sized portion at dinner for extra savings. You may also find that the vegetarian or low-carb menu offers delicious options at reasonable prices. If, despite all of your money-saving efforts, your favorite restaurant is still out of reach, enjoy its lunch menu rather than dinner menu for sizable savings. Also, always ask about daily specials. Even though "special" doesn't always mean savings, it may translate into a one-of-a-kind delicious meal for you to enjoy.

Look for the best fine dining deals around holidays. During Christmas, New Year's, Valentine's Day, St. Patrick's Day, the Fourth of July, and Thanksgiving, among other holidays, pricey restaurants will promote multiple-course meals for one price. When you add up the value of all the food and beverages you'll enjoy, it can be quite a savings. Just be sure to make your reservations early. If it's a particularly popular restaurant with limited seating, ask for a reservation even before the promotion is announced.

Moderate restaurant chains such as Chili's, Durango's, and Hops often run Christmas promotions that give you

> **Live It!**
>
> If you like earning airline miles, then you should see if your credit card is linked into the iDine promotion, a program which allows you to earn extra miles based on the restaurants you enjoy. To find out more, visit *www.idine.com*.

free gift certificates if you purchase additional gift certificates. For example, Chili's Christmas 2004 promotion was a free $5 certificate with every $20 in gift cards purchased. If you know that you will be eating at specific restaurants throughout the year and the restaurant offers this kind of deal only at Christmas, set aside some extra money in the Christmas budget to stock up on gift cards for use during the year. They are great to have on hand when cash is short or you need a birthday gift. Check the expiration dates of the free certificates given, as these promotional items are often only good for a couple of months.

A limited number of gourmet restaurants offer gift certificates on *www.skyauction.com*. Simply type in the keyword "certificates" on the search page to take a look at what offers are available. You can bid on them with a savings of 30 to 80 percent off the full retail value. For example, we bid on $100 certificates that could be used at several South Florida restaurants. The bidding began at $1 and closed with a winning bid of $51. As the winners, we had the option of buying 1 to 25 of these $100 gift certificates at a price of just $51 each, plus a $15 service charge for the entire order (not per certificate). Remember to only order as many as you would really use or give as gifts, and check the expiration dates before bidding.

The Entertainment Book, *www.entertainment.com*, which is designed for specific cities or regions, offers some fantastic deals including 2-for-1 and 50 percent-off coupons for fine dining at elegant restaurants, moderate cafes, and fast-food chains in your area. Each book also includes coupons in many other categories as well, and they are definite bargains at $20 to $30 each. In addition, clubs and frequent-diner cards are worth using—especially if you visit the restaurant on a regular basis.

When eating out, one benefit that can save money later is found in leftovers. Health experts believe that the average restaurant meal is at least twice as much food as anyone needs to consume in one meal. Ask for a to-go box and divide your meal in half. Enjoy the first half and then take the rest home for a great lunch the next day.

Finally, remember that when deciding where to eat out, five-star diners always weigh the cost and benefits. As stated before, Five-Star Living involves far more than just saving money. It also means creating precious memories; indulging in relaxing, rejuvenating activities; and making the most of every moment. Sometimes it is important to eat at home to save money for a while and then splurge with an evening out at your favorite restaurant. Take your honey, your friend, or even a great book, and make it a night to remember. Sit outside and watch the sunset, order dessert just because (with absolutely no guilt!), and refuse to talk or think about work, problems, or other things you need to get done. Fully enjoy the experience, and it will be worth any price for the sheer pleasure and stress-free relaxation it brings.

Five-Star Fact

Looking for a table upgrade? Never tip the maître d' or head waiter anything under $20. Depending on the restaurant, $50 or $100 may be more appropriate. Be discreet in your tipping. Fold the bill into a square and tuck it between your thumb and palm. When you reach out to shake the hand of the maître d', then you can quietly pass the bill. Always remember that you get what you tip for!

Gourmet Groceries and Decadent Dining

★ Buy fresh meats, veggies, and fruits in season for full flavor and affordable prices.

★ Buy in bulk and plan menus a week or month ahead.

★ Get produce at farmer's markets and local roadside stands whenever possible for better flavor and price.

★ Find new recipes in magazines and online.

★ Match coupons to weekly grocery store ads.

★ Watch for rebates, and ring rebate items separately when you check out.

★ Shop alone if you can for less frustration and impulse buys.

★ Buy gift cards when restaurants have bonus offers, and purchase coupon calendars for savings throughout the year.

★ If you do shop with kids, allow them to contribute a certain limit to the cart to avoid endless haggling over what they want.

★ Indulge yourself once in a while and make the most of every moment.

Let Us
Entertain You

I f there is one thing most people like to do, it's go out and play. With adults that are self-employed in both our families and one of us with a van filled with kids, we are constantly hunting for activities and entertainment that will fit all ages, likes and dislikes, and price ranges. We want to create memories that will last a lifetime, and what better way to do that than to have lots of fun?

Whatever we do, we need to balance our need to work with our need—yes, it is a need—to enjoy life. And so do you. Have you ever heard the question "Are you working to live or living to work?" Choose to work to live, and build in respites of fun and relaxation so that you can be filled with peace and radiate joy. Your goal should be to have others asking, "What's your secret? Why are you so happy all the time?" The answer is a life well lived.

Let's Go to the Movies

Movie watching can be a blast, but it can also be expensive. A couple of years ago, my husband and I decided to take the whole family to the local movie theater and that we would splurge on popcorn, drinks, and other snacks. The decision to go was a spontaneous one, so I didn't have time to search for deals, pull out my coupons, or try any other cost-saving techniques. We were going to go all out, and boy, did we!

The tickets were $7 each for adults and $5 each for our children. Everyone was over the age of two, so we had to buy tickets for all eight of us. That meant a ticket total of $44 before we even walked in the door. Once inside, we bought two large bags of popcorn for $9.50, two slushies for $7, four small sodas for $10, one medium soda for $3, and one large soda for $3.75. Add my husband's chocolate-covered peanuts to the pile (okay, I confess, and my Milk Duds too), and that was another $7, bringing our grand total for the movie night excursion to $84.25. And that didn't include the gas to get there and back.

Needless to say, we haven't done that again. Not that we haven't gone to the movies; we have—plenty of times. We just try to enjoy the same experience for a lot less. We aim for the afternoon matinees and "twilight" showings (usually between 4 and 6 PM), where tickets for everyone usually cost $5 or less. Or we head to the second-run cinema, where movie prices are 75¢ to $2. We joined the movie chains' reward programs, where buyers get points for every movie ticket purchased. Every 10 or 15 points (depending upon the program), we receive a coupon for a free drink, popcorn, or a free admission for later use.

You can find these savings too. In some coupon books like the Entertainment Book, you can preorder movie tickets with their special coupons that reduce the price by a couple of dollars each. When checking movie schedules online at a theater company's website, check out the home page for additional special offers, which sometimes include free popcorn, candy, drink, free kids' movies during the summertime, and extra reward points for seeing specific movies the company is promoting.

In addition to using those methods, you can also search local stores' rebate catalogs (such as Walgreens, CVS, and Target) for "movie cash" promotions, where by purchasing designated products and mailing in the rebate form with receipts and UPC codes, you will receive movie "checks" good for free admissions to any movie at most theaters in the United States. In fact, the movie cash program will reimburse the cost of your ticket if you can't find a theater near you that will accept the check. Free movie tickets for children's movies are sometimes tucked into cereal boxes or other kid-friendly foods. Do an Internet search for "free movie tickets" and see what you can find.

> **Give It!**
>
> Give your free movie tickets to a couple who needs a night out together and offer your babysitting services for free.

As far as snacks are concerned, theaters usually give free refills on large bags of popcorn and will often give you small paper bags if you ask. You can then split the big bag into the smaller bags for your kids and make use of the free refill. As part of the customer rewards program, some movie chains give free small popcorns to all rewards members on the same day each week.

In order to teach kids the value of money and to prevent over-indulging in soda, ask for complimentary ice cups and just drink water. You are not depriving yourself or your kids, as plenty of soda can be purchased for less money any other time during the day. Same goes for sweets. You should consider indulging in only one small item at the movie theater that everyone can share, or take the same money and buy a much larger quantity of snacks later.

Using those savings tips, if our family of eight goes to the movies again, the total now looks like this:

- Seven tickets at $5 each (with one ticket free from rewards points or mail-in offers)—$35
- One large popcorn—$4.75
- TOTAL—$39.75, a savings of $44.50

Movie Night In

You don't have to step foot in a theater to enjoy a quality movie experience. Renting a movie allows you to enjoy the coziness and amenities of your own home. If you prefer a night in, you can use all the extra money saved to order specialty take-out pizza or make your own at home. Enjoy sodas with microwave or air-popped popcorn. Buy ice cream and toppings to make sundaes and shakes, and you can still enjoy the experience for less than $30. You can be comfortable in your nightclothes, stop the movie if anyone needs a break, and cozy up as a family on your sofa.

Finding deals from video stores is a cinch. Watch the mailbox for local coupon books that may contain special offers. If you don't mind signing up for e-mail from the companies you frequent the most, additional coupons and savings will also turn up every few weeks in your e-mail box. Free movie rental coupons can even be found on the back of cereal or other product boxes, giving

> **Live It!**
>
> If you have a choice of video rental companies, always pick the one that doesn't charge late fees. In the long run, you'll save a ton. If your rental chain does not charge late fees, be sure to read the fine print. Under Blockbuster's policy, the company bills you for the retail price of the movie if you don't return it within a certain period of time. You don't accumulate daily late fees, but you may end up owning movies you never wanted.

you a free $4 product (the video rental) for spending $2.50 on the cereal (or $1.50, if it was bought with a coupon).

Most video store chains also offer their members reward programs. At Blockbuster, for example, the rewards program has a fee, but sometimes the company will have special promotions where the price of renewal is reduced or you receive a free gift card with your renewal. For the annual fee, you get a wealth of benefits: a coupon mailed each month for a free rental, additional free rentals with each paid rental every Monday through Wednesday, and one free rental after each five paid rentals in a single month (up to two per month).

Consequently, by using my freebies and coupons, I can spend $20 to rent five movies in a month and through the rewards program actually take home 12 movies that month using the free rentals and coupons. In addition, there are several times during the year when this chain offers a free family or kids' rental with each paid rental, bringing the total to 17 movies for $20.

Some companies also offer unlimited video rentals for a monthly subscription price. With Netflix, subscribers choose movies they want to see and receive them by mail. When they are finished, they drop them back in the mail and order more. The faster you watch and return the films, the more films you can receive in a month. Blockbuster offers the unlimited rentals too, both through the mail and in stores.

During holidays and special promotion times, look for bonus gift cards with a purchase. If you know that you will be renting movies all year long, it makes sense to buy the $50 in gift cards and get the free $5 gift card with purchase. Then you can use the gift cards as needed. If you like to buy certain movies or DVDs to own, check the video rental stores for special offers if you preorder the DVD from them. The DVD may cost more than it would at a Sam's Club or Wal-Mart, but free rentals may make it a better deal.

Good Tunes

If you enjoy your music, you're not alone. Today, you don't have to spend a ton to enjoy the latest tunes. If you prefer downloading your songs off the Internet, you'll find major chains, including Wal-Mart, competing to get your business. For under a buck a song, you can load up your iPod with everything from the latest U2 hits to classics by Frank Sinatra. To promote the transition to music downloads, a variety of companies have been giving away free downloads. Simply by checking under the cap of your soda or unwrapping a sandwich at your local fast-food place, you may find a coupon or code for the download of free songs. The songs can be stored on your home computer or laptop and burned onto CDs or transferred to portable devices that hold MP3 files. You can also find tons of MP3s from artists—especially new ones—who are willing to share their songs with you for free.

> ### *Live It!*
>
> If you have a stack of CDs you haven't listened to in a while, consider trading them in for credit at a local music exchange shop or sell them on eBay. You can use the cash to buy the albums you really want.

If you're trying to expand your CD collection, it's time to join a club. You know the offer: a dozen CDs for under a dollar (plus shipping). As long as you fulfill your obligation to buy a certain number of CDs within a certain time period, you can save hundreds of dollars on new music. Sam's Club offers low prices, especially on boxed sets, and look for under-$10 CDs from Best Buy, Circuit City, Target, and more in their weekly flyers. You can also compare prices and shop online. A quick check at *www.froogle.com* will allow you to compare prices and grab the best deal. Just make sure you read the fine print about shipping and, if possible, buy new. There's nothing worse than buying a scratched CD, even if you own a CD repair kit.

Hitting the Town

When you want to get the best entertainment bang for the buck in your own city or hometown, focus on variety and always be willing to try something different. If you've never explored the free and inexpensive tourist attractions in your own area, pack a gourmet picnic and hit the road on weekends, diving into museums, art galleries, local parks and recreation centers, and community swimming pools.

Consider visiting a local food factory to learn how products are made and sample tasty treats. If there's a chocolate, cheese, or other type of food factory in your area, take the tour. You'll enjoy the experience and learn something new.

In Florida, plenty of quality entertainment is available for little or no cost, from long walks on the beach at sunset to a quiet evening reading a favorite book, sipping a cappuccino, and listening to local performers share their talents during open mike events at local bookstores.

Christian music concerts are a bargain compared to mainstream music ticket prices, with most shows under $20 and many that are free or on a donation-only basis. Churches are also great places to socialize, with busy singles' programs, vacation Bible schools, midweek services with kids' clubs, special live entertainment nights, and other events that singles, couples, and families can enjoy while building relationships with others who share their faith and values.

One church in my area hosts the Cornerstone Café on the first Friday night of each month, where anyone in the community can stop in and watch a free, family-friendly movie projected onto their big screen while enjoying flavored coffee, soda, popcorn, chips, and homemade desserts. It even comes with nursery care provided for little ones. The church fills its sanctuary with folding tables covered with tablecloths, adds candles, and keeps the lights dim to create a great atmosphere. It's a wonderful outreach by the church to the local community and affordable fun for people who want to get out of the house but don't want a great expense.

In another city nearby, a Christian coffeehouse is open every Saturday night with live music, comedians, and other entertainment. They sell snacks at a reasonable price, and the shows are free. Search for similar programs in your area. If they aren't available, consider starting one.

If paying for a babysitter prevents you from enjoying evenings out, get together with one to three other families with children who are in the same predicament and "co-op" the child care. If four families participate, one Friday night each month would be your turn to keep all of the children at your home; and the other three Friday nights your kids would go to one of the other families' homes. Before you establish your co-op, cover the following bases:

- Make sure you have strong friendships with each other.

- Discuss whether you all have similar parenting styles and what forms of discipline can be used.

- Make sure that everyone is faithful to pick up their children at the agreed-upon time.

- Choose friends that can be counted on to take their turn to keep the kids.

- Establish whether each couple wants to go out alone or pair up with the other couples for some great fellowship.

If four nights a month is too much, find one other family and trade off every two weeks.

For educational entertainment, opportunities range from science centers and planetariums to art and historical museums. Check the venue's calendar for days when admission is free (Dads are usually free on Father's Day, Moms on Mother's Day, everyone is free on certain anniversary days, etc.). During presidential election years, political rallies can be entertaining and educational, giving you an inside glimpse of the candidate you support. The newspaper will also list upcoming talks and readings at local libraries, plus author signings at bookstores. Many clubs and organizations also meet at public facilities such as libraries. Stop in at your local branch, get a free library card if you don't already have one, and ask for a meeting calendar and a list of upcoming library events. Additionally, many libraries have meeting rooms you can sign up to use at no cost to hold your own club meetings or events.

Scan the newspaper for special entertainment offers locally and for area festivals and fund-raising events. My husband and I have enjoyed scrumptious delicacies from some of the finest restaurants in our area by attending fund-raisers for places like the local aquarium and zoo. The tickets can be pricey ($50 to $100), but we find that the price is worth it if the food is from the best restaurants, if there is live entertainment or dancing, and especially if there is a silent auction with gift certificates and other items we can purchase for less than their retail price while still donating to a worthy cause. Beyond the actual cost of the dinner (an amount the sponsor should disclose), the price of the tickets is also tax deductible as a donation to charity. At events like these, we get to dress in our finery, treat each other like royalty, and feel as though we've spent a night at the ball (a far cry from the nights spent in our pajamas in front of the TV and wonderful for the romantic at heart).

During spring and fall, local festivals provide lots of fun factor. There are seafood fests, art festivals, pumpkin festivals, Oktoberfest—you name it, some town celebrates it. Spend an afternoon enjoying beautiful weather and admiring local artwork or chowing down on lobster tails and crab legs.

When special shows like the circus, professional ice skating shows, or live syndicated children's shows (we've seen *Sesame Street Live!, Barney and Friends,* and *VeggieTales*) come to town, it pays to compare the ticket prices for different days and times. Shows often discount the opening performance or offer bonus gifts or opportunities to come early and meet the performers, giving you an extra treat for the money spent. Weekdays generally offer better prices than weekends, and many shows distribute coupons through fast-food outlets and grocery stores. AAA automobile club memberships also entitle members to discounts on tickets to many shows if purchased at a local AAA office.

If you're near the water, check out the cost of renting a boat or canoe if you don't own one, or hop on a charter boat for a fishing excursion. Ask the captain what discount you can get for putting together a group, and don't be afraid to bargain. If a boat rental or charter seems expensive, break the cost down into the hours of entertainment it provides to determine if the investment is worth it. If the boat excursion lasts two hours and costs $40, $20 an hour might not be worth the price. If the $40 is for an all-day ride, it might be well worth every penny.

You can expand your winter outdoor recreation list by trying a new sport such as skiing, snowboarding, cross-country skiing, snowshoeing, or even ice fishing. If you have a friend who offers to introduce you to a new sport, take advantage of the opportunity.

For year-round entertainment, compare prices of annual

Live It!

Four Activities for a Free Day

1. Bake homemade cookies from scratch. Invite friends over to enjoy the tasty treats or deliver them to neighbors and coworkers.

2. Attend a free event in your town. Is there a local author reading or musician playing at a bookstore? Check the newspaper for activities.

3. Spend an afternoon at the flea market. Look at antiques and knickknacks. Enjoy the opportunity to browse and relax.

4. Turn your home into a spa. Invite some friends over for manicures, pedicures, and facials.

and seasonal memberships to theater companies, museums, and local attractions. Find out if the membership also gives you access to similar venues nationwide. For example, a membership to the local zoo usually includes entry to all the other member zoos in the United States. A family membership to the science center might give you and the kids access to most science centers around the nation. Our family wanted to have a membership to the big science centers in our area but did not want to pay the $130 family membership price. I went online and looked at the cost of annual memberships to other reciprocating science centers. A center in another city in Florida, coincidentally named the Gillespie Museum (I am not kidding), had a family membership for $35. I mailed in the application with my $35 check, received my cards in the mail, and am now a card-carrying member of a museum that not only bears my last name, but also gives me free admission to the science centers in Tampa and Orlando at a fraction of the big-city fees. (Visit *www.astc.org* for a list of participating science centers.)

When we purchased our annual membership cards to Weeki Wachee, the roadside attraction that is home to Florida's famous mermaid show and a water park that kids love, it also included free admission for the year to the Florida Aquarium, the Mote Marine Aquarium, Homosassa Springs, and the Lowry Park Zoo, a savings of more than $400 if we visited each of those places just *one time* during the year. The annual cards were only $40 each, about what it cost for two individual admissions to the park.

For more active fun, consider joining the YMCA if it has facilities you will use and enjoy. The cost is usually less expensive than joining a gym, and the YMCA offers children's and teen classes and activities, mother-and-child classes, exercise and performing arts classes, sports teams, and often a pool. The Y even has a scholarship program that reduces the monthly fee for families who qualify based on income level. Best of all, the YMCA is founded on biblical principles, and you can feel good about supporting an organization that gives back to the families in your community.

Some of the most hilarious outings we have had as a family are bowling nights. Bowling alleys have different specials daily and sometimes give free games to kids during the summer, a free game for every game that you pay for, free shoes with the price of a game, and other deals. It's an activity that almost any age can enjoy. I would strongly advise checking out the alleys in your area before you decide to play. Some lanes at night are not kid-friendly atmospheres (and are often filled with cigarette smoke). If a slower-paced game is more your style, get in the car and go miniature golfing. When adults ask my husband about his golf handicap, he smiles and says he can get it through the windmill every time! Miniature golf courses are affordable, and coupons are often included in local circulars, newspapers, and entertainment coupon books.

Give It!

Ready to try something new? The National Park Service looks for volunteers through its website at *www.nps.gov/volunteer*. A few of the positions even include food, housing, or transportation reimbursement. Consider getting involved today!

If you enjoy live sports events, they are abundant in most communities, from local high school football, baseball, and basketball games that are free or cost a couple dollars entry fee to high-dollar professional sports events. To get the thrill of fast-paced action without paying professional sports ticket prices, consider attending college games in your area. Tickets can be ordered through the colleges or universities for individual games or, for more savings, the whole season. Pay attention to newspaper classified ads, and pick up a campus newspaper to find tickets that students want to sell at reduced prices.

For the professional sports lover, the cost is higher; but bargains can still be had. Watch the newspaper for certain game specials, such as reduced ticket prices or free snacks with the ticket price. Go online and look at your favorite team's schedule and search for advertised deals on its site. If season passes offer a cost savings but are still too pricey, find a friend (or several) who might want to split the season with you. You all split the cost of the season tickets and divvy them up equally.

Live theater is another enjoyable pastime, from local community theater to national Broadway tours. Community theaters offer the best value, but the production quality can be hit-and-miss. Visit a few theaters or ask around to discover which ones offer the types of shows and quality you desire at the price that fits your budget. Look for opening night ticket specials, and ask the theater if they do preview nights (generally the dress rehearsal the night before a show opens) for free or a reduced price. Weekend matinees also offer generous discounts over the weekend evening shows. For students of any age with proper college identification, most theaters give a discounted ticket rate. For theatergoers (sometimes limited to students only) willing to wait in line at the last minute, unsold seats may be released an hour or two before showtime at an extremely discounted price. You have to count

Live It!

Have you ever considered attending special, one-of-a-kind annual events in small towns around your community? If you happen to live near Liberal, Kansas, you can enjoy the annual International Pancake Day. If you are near Metropolis, Illinois, you can put on a mask and cape and attend the Superman Celebration with thousands of other fans.

Five-Star Fact

Planning a trip to the Big Apple? You can find reduced last-minute tickets to Broadway shows at the TKTS booth in the center of Times Square. If you want to buy in advance, consider joining organizations such as Audience Extras (AE), Play by Play, and Theatermania.com's Gold Club. You may have to pay an annual membership fee, but you'll be given offers on reduced-price Broadway and Off Broadway shows. Also check out *www.playbill.com*.

★ ★ ★ ★ ★

the cost of your time and be willing to be disappointed if you wait in line and there are no tickets left. Think of this technique as similar to flying standby. Sometimes you will get on the flight you want; sometimes you won't.

Big-name concerts, even sold-out shows, also usually release previously unavailable seats just an hour or two before a show. While the tickets may not be discounted, you can get some of the best seats in the house (usually reserved for band members' family and friends who are not coming after all) at the last minute. Look for grand-opening specials at auditoriums. The new amphitheater in Tampa recently offered tickets to every fall show—from Sting and Annie Lennox to Ozzfest to Michael W. Smith with MercyMe—for $10 each on one particular day (with a limit of four tickets per purchase). The lines were horrendous, but, for many, the thrill of winning the equivalent of a small lottery (some Sting tickets sell for upward of $100 each) was well worth the wait—and actually part of the adventure.

> ### Live It!
>
> Got a favorite band or musician? Check out the artist's website. A number of musicians have street teams—a group of people who are committed to promoting an album or upcoming event. In exchange for putting up posters and promoting the musician through word of mouth, you can score discount concert tickets, free CDs, and even the occasional backstage pass.

You can also volunteer for fun. It may sound odd at first, but volunteering for a local charity or event can be loads of entertainment. If you have special events coming to your town—whether it's a race, festival, or concert—get involved. You can use your time and talents, make new friends, and enjoy yourself.

Finally, for entertainment that will pay off for a lifetime, spend some time each year doing things you have always wanted to do. Whether it is making a quilt with the local quilting club or traveling across the state to embark on a dolphin-watching cruise, everyone deserves to fill their lives at least occasionally with the pure excitement that comes with living life to the fullest. It's what we were created to do. Something that seems expensive in terms of the dollars it will cost may be worth every penny if it is a once-in-a-life-time five-star opportunity that will keep paying you in joy every time you remember it.

Let Us Entertain You

★ Utilize customer rewards programs.

★ Watch for free movie tickets and video rental coupons on products you normally buy, especially kids' products.

★ Know which days of the week offer special deals (free popcorn at the movies, extra video rentals, special seats to circuses and ice shows).

★ Familiarize yourself with local entertainment venues and auditoriums to choose the best seats for the price you can afford.

★ Pick up tickets at the box office rather than using online services that charge a handling fee per ticket and shipping costs.

★ Take advantage of the best local free sites and activities your area has to offer.

★ Do your homework to find packages and entertainment specials before you head out the door.

★ Look for grand opening specials.

★ Find friends willing to "co-op" babysitting, season tickets, and the like.

★ Seek out unique experiences everywhere you go, something you could only do or see in that locale.

★ Enjoy simple things such as family nights with a board game (that's board, not bored) or a game of charades or improvisation.

★ Schedule activities you have always wanted to do.

The World As Your Oyster

There's something addictive about traveling. The more we do it, the more we want to do it. Sure, it's exhausting, frustrating, and harrowing at times, but something about traveling to new places makes you feel so alive. Maybe it's the adventure, encountering the unknown, meeting new people, or just the idea of trying something different. Whatever the cause, when there is an opportunity to go someplace new, we're always game. Travel deals are plentiful for both business trips and pleasure jaunts—from great hotel buys in fabulous cities to airline deals that can knock hundreds off your trip's pricetag. The key to finding the five-star deals is spending some time to research and preplan as much as you can.

Ultimate Vacations

Is there some place you have wanted to visit your whole life, but you are not sure you can figure out how to line everything up so you can actually go? Your Ultimate Vacation could be right around the corner if you make up your mind to take the time to do it and then start planning your strategy to make it happen. Maybe you want to climb Machu Picchu, raft down the Grand Canyon, or hike into the Amazon. Perhaps your idea of fun is found aboard a luxurious cruise ship. Or how about embarking on an African safari, sailing down the Yangtze River in China on a houseboat, or attending the Oscars?

Ultimate Vacations should be once-in-a-lifetime experiences, trips you will always remember.

My Ultimate Vacation story began around Thanksgiving 2003, when I discovered that the 7 UP company was auctioning off trips to the Grammy awards in Los Angeles for points that could be accumulated by buying 7 UP products. I watched the Internet site closely to see how many points the vacations were going for, and calculated how much soda I would have to buy. With a green light from my husband, who loves me even though I can go off on some pretty wild tangents, I bought about $500 worth of 7 UP products, entered the codes online, and began accumulating points. Even with cases of soda stacked in my garage, I didn't come close to winning.

Now I was out $500, and my kids were on a constant sugar high. The first weekend in December, my husband joined some other guys in our family for a football weekend in New Orleans (his Ultimate Vacation). After he left, I figured he was going to spend more than $500 on his trip, so maybe I would buy more soda and try again, since 7 UP had another set of the trips online. I spent the weekend collecting 12-packs from all the convenience stores in my county and beyond (at one chain of stores, they were going for only $1.99 each). I logged the codes in faithfully for hours, and Sunday night I bid on the trip all night long.

I had plenty of points this time, and I was determined to

win. Well, somewhere right before 6 AM, I closed my eyes for just a minute. When I came to, the auction was over. I could have outbid the winner with my points, but my chance was gone!

Now the tally was $1200 in soda, my husband was coming home, and I had an even fuller garage, emptier wallet, and no trip. Fortunately, my husband is an incredible guy; and he didn't even blink twice. At that point, I had no idea if 7 UP would even auction off another set of trips, as it was now December and the Grammys were in early February. But that week they offered one last trip. I bid and rebid, and at 3 AM December 15, I won. Let me tell you, it was worth all the effort!

My $1200 trip to the Grammys included airfare for my husband and me from Tampa, Florida, to Los Angeles, California, limousine service to and from the airport, two nights at a luxurious downtown hotel, shuttle service to the Grammys, $600 in American Express checks, two tickets to the Grammy awards (unavailable to the public), and a variety of 7 UP souvenirs. I even had some extra points leftover that I used to win a backstage rehearsal tour of the Grammys, where we toured the press room, the green carpet, and watched Foo Fighters and Outkast rehearse. Oh, and my extra points also scored me an oversized, bright orange Sunkist beach towel. (Hey, it's a great prize for a family that lives in Florida!)

It was such a crazy experience that the *St. Petersburg Times* came out and did a little story on us and took a picture of my kids perched atop a pyramid of soda. To complete the five-star experience and fulfill the Live It! Give It! principles, we donated a lot of the soda to our youth group at church, and the youth sold it as a fund-raiser before church dinners.

While not every vacation can be purchased with soda points, Ultimate Vacation deals are around every corner. Whether you are just taking a family weekend away or are hopping a flight for a business trip, you can plan ahead and secure some amazing deals that allow you to get the best sleep and the most enjoyment every time you leave your home. We, perhaps like you, are past the years of being able to crash on someone's couch at a moment's notice and still get a good night's sleep. Something strange happens to stomachs that live off of fast food and sleep on uncomfortable mattresses for too many nights in a row. We can still do it if we have to, but we'd rather not. If you need comfort and prefer class, you—like us—are in the position of trying to land that four- or five-star deal on a two- or three-star budget.

The good news is that it's possible! You can stay in nice hotels at a fraction of the cost. You can stop in places that offer full kitchens, extra cushy beds, or full-service amenities without overspending. It takes a little extra research, some flexibility, and savvy shopping, but at the end of your trip it's always worth it.

Sky-High Airline Deals

Airline tickets can consume a good chunk of anyone's travel budget, so if you're going to save money on your next vacation, you need to begin with where and how you purchase your tickets. You can always go to a travel agent, but you just might find you can do better on your own if you go online—especially after you deduct the service fee.

The three basic rules of saving money on airline tickets are:

1. Fly midweek.

2. Book at least 21 days in advance.

3. Be flexible in your dates and times.

These rules seem simple and obvious, but they aren't always possible—especially if your best friend just had a baby and you need to be on a plane in the next 48 hours. If you're flexible about your arrival and departure times, there's usually no better place than *www.priceline.com*, which will allow you to bid on a ticket—selecting both the arrival and departure cities as well as the date—but won't reveal the airline or the times of the flights until the bid is accepted and you've paid for it. I've used Priceline a number of times, and I've ended up on some pretty wacky flights, leaving at 6 AM and arriving toward midnight, which wasn't always convenient if a friend or family member was planning to pick me up at the airport. However, I've also gotten some pretty amazing deals.

One February I decided to make a last-minute decision to run the L.A. marathon. I had been training, but I wasn't sure whether or not I was up for the 26.2-mile trek. Within the 21-day limit, I couldn't find a ticket from Denver for less than $250, but with a quick bid on Priceline I landed the ticket for $137—a savings of $113.

You can bid any amount on a Priceline ticket, but it's generally a good rule of thumb to start at a third of the retail price and work your way higher, based on the amount of time you want to spend rebidding.

At a certain point, you may just want to go with a known carrier and flight time, but only you can decide your threshold. One of the best features of Priceline is that if your bid is in the ballpark of an acceptable offer, the website will counteroffer with a price. It's your choice to accept it or not, but you'll know you have your ticket if you take it.

The website, *www.biddingfortravel.com,* is an independent site designed specifically to help give Priceline shoppers bidding strategy. Message boards contain information on recently accepted bids, counteroffers, and prices on various travel itineraries. Always give the site a quick scan, and if you have time, post your desired route. If you decide to use their information, as a courtesy, link to Priceline through their site so they can be acknowledged for promoting the Web traffic.

Another bidding option is Hotwire, *www.hotwire.com*, which acts a lot like Priceline if you're flexible in your travel times. The site adds a small surcharge for each ticket. Whichever bidding site you choose, make sure you double-check your information before you press "bid." I recently shopped for a ticket from Colorado to Minnesota. I wasn't sure whether it would be less expensive to fly out of Colorado Springs or Denver, so I bid the same amount on both and was denied. I decided to bid again, and I was both surprised and delighted when I landed the ticket for $200, half the price being quoted on other websites. I was excited until I realized that I had accidentally purchased a roundtrip ticket from Colorado Springs to Denver! I spent the next hour calling Hotwire, waiting on hold, and explaining the situation. They verified my bidding history and a very kind agent was willing to refund the money minus the $75 change fee required by the airline. They told me I would never be given another chance to change a reservation.

> **Live It!**
>
> Tired of being crunched in a middle seat for a four-hour cross-country flight? You can find the best seats at *www.seatexpert.com* or *www. seatguru.com*, two websites that help you identify the most comfortable seats on an aircraft.

If you have a set time that you need to arrive or depart, then you are going to want to visit a website that offers you all the details before you make your purchase. There are a number to choose from, including:

- *www.cheaptickets.com*
- *www.statravel.com*
- *www.travel.yahoo.com*
- *www.orbitz.com*
- *www.lowestairprice.com*
- *www.sidestep.com*
- *www.travelocity.com*
- *www.expedia.com*
- *www.qixo.com*
- *www.cheapseatstravel.com*
- *www.lowestfare.com*

Our favorites are *www.orbitz.com*, *www.qixo.com*, and *www.cheaptickets.com*. Usually the prices are comparable, within $30 of each other, but occasionally you will find one with a significantly better deal. Most websites allow you to decide whether you are willing to take a nondirect or a red-eye flight, and if you're a night owl and willing to live with the inconvenience, you can shave 10 to 40 percent off your ticket price. Every website has a different policy and different fees that they attach to the total cost of your airline ticket. Make sure your total includes all website fees and government and security taxes, as well as any other charges, to avoid unwanted surprises. Also, double-check the price of a ticket directly from the major airlines themselves. I have found that some of the travel "deals" on Expedia or Orbitz were actually the same fare the airline itself offered, *plus* a $5 or $10 service fee.

Before you get to the airport, you will want to make sure your luggage doesn't tip the scales past 50 pounds. If you think it might, try weighing it on your bathroom scale before you fly. If you have an awkward-sized bag, simply weigh yourself, and then step on the scale holding the bag and subtract the difference. If you think you may be coming home with some large or heavy souvenirs, pack an extra duffel bag inside of your suitcase. This little addition can save you extra fees.

Landing in First Class

Finding yourself in first class without paying the full fare required can be challenging, but it's not impossible. Some people recommend asking the gate agent—with your biggest, friendliest smile—if an upgrade is available. Occasionally this works, but more often than not you'll find yourself to be the fourth person to ask the question in the last 15 minutes.

A better route? If you haven't already, you need to sign up for all the promotions and discounts available from your favorite airlines. Over the last year, I've received first-class upgrade certificates from Northwest Airlines, Alaska Airlines,

Five-Star Fact

Operating a small plane can be expensive. That's why some private pilots are looking for people to share the expense via *www.flyshare.com*. It can be difficult to match up itineraries, but you never know when a private pilot may be headed in the right direction. Just be sure to ask about the person's flight record!

★ ★ ★ ★ ★

and United Airlines. Some of the certificates require a certain class of ticket (aka more expensive, non-restricted fare), but others are more flexible.

Another option for landing a first-class seat is to join a frequent flyer program and do your best to stay loyal to that program. American Airlines and Alaska Airlines have had programs that entitle elite or MVP members to receive free upgrades to first class if they're available. In addition, both airlines have offered individual programs whereby customers can buy upgrades to first class in $50 increments based on the mileage (AirTran has offered upgrades for $35). For example, a ticket that covers between 1–1250 miles may cost you $50 to upgrade to first class while one between 1250–2500 may cost you $100. Many promotional offers are only available the day of the flight, but they're still worth checking out.

A Friendly Bump

My husband and I recently set a new personal record for collecting bump tickets. We were on our way home from Phoenix, Arizona, and we had a hunch that the airline was oversold, so we got to the airport two and a half hours early and cleared security. We went straight to the gate and offered to volunteer. The agent said she wasn't sure she needed anyone, but we encouraged her to put our names down just in case. It turned out she needed two volunteers, and we were at the top of the list. She rebooked us on a flight that left two hours later, handed us two tickets for anywhere in the U.S., Canada, and Mexico that the airline flew, and went off to work another gate.

We waited for the agents who were handling our new flight to arrive, and we asked them if they needed any volunteers. The agent said they were overbooked and put our names on a list. When the flight was ready to leave, the agent gave us an option to volunteer, but it would require spending the night in Phoenix and covering our own hotel expenses. We looked at each other, smiled, and said "that's fine." We now had four tickets for anywhere the airline flew in North America.

I had a friend from junior high I hadn't seen in many years that I had hoped to visit while we were in the area. I gave her a quick call and accepted the invitation to stay in her guest room. Then we went to the rental car area in the airport, found an off-brand rental car for $18 a day, added an extra $4 a day for a midsized, more comfortable vehicle, and spent a nostalgic day with my friend.

The next morning we got up early and headed to the airport. Again, we went straight to the gate, and through the same process as the previous morning. We collected two more free tickets. We were set to accept another bump on the second flight of the morning except for one glitch. The gate agent was the same as the first flight, and she wasn't going to let us bump from flight to flight. We had to get on board.

By delaying our arrival home, we collected a total of six airline

Give It!

Most airlines have programs which allow you to donate miles to needy, underprivileged, and terminally ill children. Families adopting children from foreign countries can also use donated miles to help them afford the cost of bringing their new baby home. Consider donating miles to make a difference in someone's life.

Live It!

If you find yourself faced with a long layover due to a bump or because of an airline delay, don't let it get you down. Instead of feeling frustrated, count the downtime as extra time to relax with a book you have been wanting to read, visit with an old friend you have been meaning to call—or if the layover is really long, hop in a cab or rent a car for a few hours (a one-day rental can sometimes cost less than $15) and drive around the city. Make the most of every moment. That's Five-Star Living!

tickets with a full retail value between $3600 to $6000. Not bad for one day's work. Of course, they were nontransferable and had to be used within 12 months of the date of issue, but we still managed to use them all.

As smooth as the story may sound, I have to admit that there was some planning that went into securing the bump tickets. Here are some insider's tips:

- You need to know if any of your flights are over-booked. How can you find out? First, call the airline. Officially, an airline can't tell you if your flight is overbooked, but if you find a friendly agent you can gracefully ask whether it would be worth your time to get to the airport early in case they need volunteers. If you can't get any help over the phone, then you should ask the agent as soon as you check in.

- Get to the airport early. You can try to volunteer at the initial check-in, which means that even if you use a kiosk for your e-ticket you still need to talk to an agent. Depending on your airline, the agent may be able to put you on a volunteer list from her computer, but most of the time they will refer you to the gate agent.

- Get your name on the volunteer list. As soon as you clear security, go straight to the gate agent and ask if they need volunteers. If they say they aren't sure, but they will make an announcement, ask if they will at least put your name on the list. If the agent who checked you in and put you on the volunteer list leaves, double-check with the new agent to make sure you're on her list. Sometimes the lists don't transfer, and even if they do, you want the agent to be able to match your name with a friendly face.

- Be cool. Agents have to deal with pushy, overly ag-gressive, and angry people all day. Make kindness your priority. Walk up slowly. Smile. Make your

request and then move out of the way. There's probably a line of people behind you that still needs to
be dealt with.

• Stay near the gate. As the boarding time approaches,
you need to be ready to stay and ready to go at the
same time. It's not the time to go shopping, use the
bathroom, or buy a snack. If they call your name
for a volunteer spot and you don't answer, they'll go
right down the list.

Even if you follow all these steps, you still may not land
a ticket. But if you do follow them, your odds will greatly increase. Last Christmas, my husband and I were flying out of
Miami on December 27. We knew the flight was overbooked
and we had a good chance at landing a ticket, so we showed
up at the airport four hours early. It was a little excessive, especially since it was an hour before the ticket agents opened
to check people in for the flight. Surprisingly, when we ar-
rived, there were already people in line. Fortunately, my husband is a frequent flyer, so we were able to get in a special
priority line. When the woman checked us in, we immediately asked if she needed volunteers. She put us down on
the list. The woman in the line beside us heard the request
and asked that her name be added to the list. Four hours
later, when the flight took off, the airline only needed two
volunteers—and my husband and I were selected simply because we volunteered first. We were each given a free ticket
anywhere in the United States and put on a flight that left an
hour and a half later.

All Those Miles Really Do Add Up

In the movie *Punch-Drunk Love*, Barry Egan (Adam
Sandler) finds a loophole in a Healthy Choice frequent flyer
promotion that allows him to earn 1,000,000 frequent flyer
miles by purchasing $3000 worth of pudding. This funny,

quirky scenario propels the idea that maybe frequent flyer miles really are the new commodity. Anyone who regularly uses frequent flyer miles realizes that Barry Egan, though fictitious, stumbled upon a goldmine. Fortunately, there really are stashes of frequent flyer miles just waiting to be mined.

If you travel a lot for work or even pleasure and use multiple carriers, it's easy to begin to think that all those frequent flyer miles won't amount to much. Don't be tricked! They will add up to something, it just may take a little savvy maneuvering to get you there.

Live It!

On some airlines, bump tickets or volunteer tickets actually have a higher priority when it comes to booking a reservation than using frequent flyer miles. So if you are trying to book a ticket with frequent flyer miles and there aren't any available flights, use one of your free bump tickets—you just may get the seat.

The first step in gathering frequent flyer miles is to join every airline's program. Even if you only think you'll fly them once, go ahead and join. Your next trip or your next client who requires a visit just might surprise you.

Whenever you're flying, study the back pages of the airline magazine usually located in the pocket of the airline seat in front of you. You'll usually find lots of information about airline partners. For example, in 2005, American Airlines was partnered with nearly two-dozen different airlines, including Delta, Continental, Alaska Airlines, Qantas, Hawaiian Airlines, and Aer Lingus, which means that whether you are traveling to New Zealand, Hawaii, or Ireland, you could still be earning thousands of miles. To collect miles on partner airlines, you have to enter your American Airlines code when you're flying them.

You also need to sign up for the e-newsletters that will keep you up to date on the latest offers. Last winter I was scheduled to take two business trips on American Airlines. Because I am a partner of Alaska Airlines and American Airlines, I knew I could have the miles attributed to either account. I did a quick check of both airlines' websites and discovered that Alaska Airlines was having a special "Codeshare Promotion" with American Airlines. So instead of giving American Airlines my American Airlines frequent flyer number, I gave them my Alaska Airlines frequent flyer number and earned double miles on both flights. That added up to nearly 8000 bonus miles or a third of a free airline ticket.

In addition to earning free miles from actually flying, you can earn tens of thousands of miles through partner promotions. Credit cards—which offer one or more miles per dollar spent—are a quick, efficient way to earn miles. While they usually have an annual fee, they can be worth the added expense. Hotels often provide frequent flyer miles, so don't forget to ask when you check in. Some hotels allow you to earn both points (on their promotion) and frequent flyer miles. Car rental companies also partner with most major airlines to earn miles, but beware of surcharges that force you to buy the miles. On a recent car rental, I was offered 50 frequent flyer miles per day, but I had to pay for them. When I did the math, it simply didn't add up.

Your favorite airlines also work with all kinds of companies to secure your business and loyalty by offering frequent flyer miles. You can earn miles through florists, charities, dining, financial services, stock purchases, and even through mortgaging your home. Retail purchases, including magazine subscriptions and name-brand clothing stores, can help you earn bonus miles.

Avoid buying something simply because it offers free miles. Frequent flyer miles should be seen as a bonus to your purchase rather than a motivating factor. If you find yourself buying products you don't need or paying more for products just because you'll earn an extra 500 miles, you need to think again.

Standby, Change Fees, and Other "Extras"

Before purchasing airline tickets, do your homework and find out the airline's standby and change fees policies. There are always special circumstances that may delay a trip, or you may be enjoying your vacation destination so much that you want to stay another day. Consider the change fee as one factor when making your buying decision. Some airlines charge $50 to $100 per change, some charge the difference in price between what you paid and what the flight you are trying to get on currently costs (which can be astronomical), and some let you change for free as long as you are willing to fly standby on the flight you want.

Check airlines' special programs for seniors and students, and you may receive a discounted fare or the chance to fly standby at a reduced rate. AirTran, for example, has had a program for anyone between the ages of 18 and 22. The X-Fares Standby Program has allowed anyone in that age bracket to fly standby to any city where AirTran flies for $55 per segment, or $75 for long-haul segments. Young adults just show up at the AirTran Airways ticket counter, put their names on the X-Fare standby list, pay for each flight segment, and go to the gate and wait to be placed on the flight.

If you have a family member in another city who has died or has a medical emergency and you need to get a quick flight out, ask the airlines about their funeral fares and emergency policies. Sometimes the fares are still very high but better than buying a ticket within 24 hours of flying.

Finally, to get the most out of your flying experience, investigate which airlines you prefer to fly. Which ones have the most leg room? The funniest or friendliest employees? Delta Air Lines has been known to offer gourmet cookies on morning flights, but some Delta Song flights offer the cookies, satellite TV, and a music trivia interactive game you can play on the back of every seat. Five-Star Living for you may mean paying a few extra dollars to get the service and amenities that make the experience the most enjoyable.

Lodging

Once you get to where you're going, you need a place to stay. When it comes to lodging, some of the best places to stay at the best prices can be found in package deals. If you're bidding on Priceline or Hotwire, you can select a "package option" that will show you the hotel you can stay at for one set rate. Often these are great deals! You can also select your hotel's rating. While five-star hotels can be hard to come by, four-star and four-and-a-half-star hotels are frequently available.

While *www.hotels.com* can offer some solid rates, you'll still want to check standby sites including *www.travelocity.com*, *www.expedia.com*, and *www.orbitz.com*. Two often overlooked but highly valuable sites when it comes to finding a hotel deal are *www.qixo.com* and *www.quikbook.com*. Other sites worth visiting include *www.bookingbuddy. com*, *www.cheapflights.com*, *www. sidestep.com*, and *www.kayak.com*. They allow you to learn about your hotel and all of the amenities before you make a payment.

One of our favorite hotel chains is the Wyndham. While the quality of hotels vary from location to location, they have a program called "Wyndham by Request," which allows you to select everything from the type of pillow you prefer—feather or foam—to the type of snack—soda and pretzels or wine and cheese—you would like waiting in your room at no extra charge. In addition, their website offers outstanding promotions and last-minute

> ### Live It!
>
> When you select a package option with Hotwire, normally you must accept whatever flight option the company chooses (on the days you specified). The flight times are not revealed until after you have locked in your purchase. However, Hotwire now shows you the available flight options for a small extra fee. For $15 to $20 more (in some cases, it's higher), you can choose the specific flights you want and still get a very good deal.

deals. Last Christmas, we were able to stay at two different Wyndham hotels—one in Miami and another in Seattle—for less than $40 a night.

In addition to price, there are a few factors to consider when selecting a hotel:

- *Additional costs.* The hotel we stayed in while working together on this project charged $20 a day for parking. Because the hotel is located near the metro, we decided we didn't need a car to get around town, but such charges need to be considered when making a reservation.

- *Age.* Find out how old your hotel is. Quality varies widely, even within the same chains of hotels. Newer buildings look better, smell better, and just feel nicer. They also usually offer better business amenities. A newer hotel in a three-star ranked chain can be much nicer than the older four-star down the street.

- *High-speed or wireless Internet access and phone calls.* It can be difficult to find out how much hotels charge for these two services unless you call them directly, but if these services are offered at no charge, it's easy to find out because the hotels will advertise this free perk! Look for chains, loyalty programs, and locations that throw in these kinds of extras—especially if you have work to do on your trip.

- *Free meals.* High-end hotels are more likely to charge for everything—from local phone calls to expensive room service. Midlevel chains like Marriott's Fairfield and Residence Inns offer complimentary breakfasts, and some also have free weeknight "social hours" with complimentary beverages and snacks. If you will be out of the room from early morning until late night, these freebies may not be a plus. But if you are going to be around, a free breakfast every morning can save you from $5 to $15 a day.

- *Location.* If your hotel is hard to get to or a long way from the airport or your final destination, you may be better off staying in a different hotel or a different part of town altogether.

- *Suites vs. a regular room.* If you want to have the extra comforts of home, suites offer more room, a separate work area from the sleeping area, and a kitchenette or full kitchen so you can bring food into your room and cook it (or at least heat it up).

When you're looking for a place to stay, a top site that shouldn't be missed is SkyAuction, *www.skyauction.com.* The website allows you to bid on travel packages as well as individual airline tickets, hotels, and rental cars. You need to read the fine print as to any extra charges, including the fee the website tags onto the cost, but you can find some incredible deals. SkyAuction allows bidders to compete for unsold timeshare rentals, airline tickets, and cruises at sometimes ridiculously low prices.

Through SkyAuction, our family has been able to enjoy five-star time-share facilities for less than $30 per night for two- to four-bedroom condos. Time-share properties are ideal for families because they include planned activities for kids and adults (from karaoke nights to scavenger hunts to limbo contests), lots of pools, washers and dryers in each unit, full kitchens with cookware, whirlpool tubs in the master bedrooms, and lots of extra amenities.

A disadvantage of hotels is that many of them don't offer a

Give It!

Wherever you stay, consider tipping the housekeeper a few dollars each day. Housekeepers' schedules vary, so it's not a good idea to wait until the end of your stay to tip because a different person may be cleaning your room on the final day of the visit than the previous ones. Housekeepers work hard—I know, because I've been one—and if you tip them, you usually get extra service with a smile. You may find surprises—from extra hand towels and soaps to extra mints on your pillow—for your graciousness. More importantly, you will help recognize a job well done and encourage someone whose work is often unappreciated.

full kitchen—which can save you money and extra weight gain when you're traveling. If you're traveling with friends, you may want to consider renting a house together and sharing the cost or finding an unused timeshare. One helpful site is *www. tug2.com*. Under classified ads, you can find a listing of available time-shares to rent or buy at a fraction of the cost.

Live It!

Traveling alone? Every solo traveler knows about the single-supplement fee. Rather than cut the fare in half, they add a surcharge to the single rate. To avoid these surcharges, consider visiting a travel matching website such as *www.travelchums. com* or *www.singlestravelintl. com*. You can also check out the Solo Travel Network (*cstn.org*).

In search of a much-needed vacation spot, my husband and I decided that we wanted to stay in a five-star, all-inclusive resort where we wouldn't have to think or worry about anything for an entire week. Through *www.tug2. com*, we found someone who was willing to part with a membership coupon to a five-star resort for $50, plus membership rates. For a week, we enjoyed all meals, beverages, non-motorized vehicles, airport transfers, and day trips, as well as a manicure, pedicure, and massage for $240 per day for both of us. The total cost for the week was $1680 plus $50. When I called the resort directly, the week priced out at $2310—a savings of $580. Using bump tickets from an earlier trip and MVP status on the airlines which allowed us to fly first class for free meant that $1730 included everything for the trip!

If you feel comfortable having strangers in your home, you can participate in a home exchange or a hospitality exchange. For a reasonable fee, a home exchange allows you to stay in exotic homes in places such as the Caribbean and Europe while your home exchange partner stays in your home. In a hospitality exchange, you host each other in your homes at designated times. Through this program, your home exchange partners stay with you as guests. Later, you stay with them as their guests. If your home has multiple bedrooms, this may be the way to go. You'll be around, so if your guest can't figure out how to work the satellite television or turn on the microwave, you can help.

Car Rental

Bidding online for car rental is probably the safest, best bet when it comes to saving money on renting a car. You can select the dates, times, and pick-up location—the only variable is the car company. So you'll find some great deals by bidding at *www.hotwire.com* or *www.priceline.com*.

If you're just not a bidding person, then it's best to price out a car online and then call them directly to avoid paying website fees. I'll often use *www.orbitz.com* to find the best rental price and then visit *www.google.com* and type in the name of the lowest priced company and the word "coupon." You can find all kinds of coupon codes to lower your price. Many of them will require you to book through that car rental company's website, but it's still worth it. For additional discounted rates and coupons, check your professional memberships, AAA, Entertainment Book, and employer for corporate rates and upgrades.

If you can't find any coupons or discounts online, then it's time to call the company. You can find the number by clicking on the "shuttle information" button from your search at *www.orbitz.com,* which provides a telephone number directly into the company's offices. Once you call, ask if they offer any discounts for AARP, Sam's Club, Costco, or other memberships. You can usually trim an extra five to ten percent off your bill. Occasionally, the prices available online will still be better.

In order to save more money, consider renting from an off-brand company, which often charges less to undercut

> ### Live It!
>
> Check out *www.tripadvisor.com* before you book any hotel room to read reviews from people who have just stayed there. It can help you avoid hotels with substandard service, rooms, or amenities.

their competitors. Also, when at all possible, rent from companies that aren't on airport property and don't have to tag on airport surcharges and fees.

Don't forget to use all those upgrade, free weekend day, and discount coupons you've been sent over the last year. They come from all kinds of sources, including credit card bills, bank statements, and direct mailings, and they can help you get a better deal.

One important thing to remember in renting cars is that smaller is not always better. Yes, you will save on gas by renting a smaller car, but there is also something to be said for comfort. Not only do you need to be able to ride comfortably, but also you need to consider how much luggage and how many kids you have to fit in your rental car. On one occasion, my kids ended up sitting with bags under their feet and between them, which made them grouchy and increased all of our stress levels. The additional $5 or $10 a day for a bigger car would have provided a true five-star experience well worth the additional cost.

When checking prices on rental cars, look for the lowest compact car price, then calculate the cost of the upgrades. When it's only a couple of dollars a day to upgrade to a more comfortable vehicle, choose the larger car. If it's $10 to $15 more a day to upgrade, book the reservation for the compact car. When the agent checks you in at the rental car counter, ask again about the cost of an upgrade. Agents are often encouraged to sell upgrades, and they will often offer them for a smaller fee, if the car is available, to get you in it.

One of the ways car rental companies make money is through insurance and gasoline—two options you will be presented with at the time of rental. Depending upon which credit card you use, the credit company may provide car rental insurance. But it's important to know what and how much of an accident they'll cover. It's also important to find out if you're covered for the days the rental car is not in use. In other words, your credit card or personal car insurance policy may cover all repairs, but you'll still be charged the full amount of the car rental rate for the days it's out of service. If it takes three weeks to schedule a repair, you could be looking at a hefty bill.

You'll also want to think twice before you return the car with a gasoline gauge on anything but full. A number of companies offer to fill up your tank at a set price per gallon, but only if from the half full or empty gauge. In reality, you'll never have your car exactly on half full or empty when you return it, and you'll find yourself paying excess gas charges. If, however, you're renting the car in a remote location—with no gas stations nearby—it may be worth the extra expenditure.

> ### Live It!
>
> Looking for a deal on luggage? The Unclaimed Baggage Center (*www.unclaimedbaggage.com*) in Scottsboro, Alabama, offers all kinds of luggage and all kinds of items people have left behind on airlines for 30 to 80 percent off.

Don't Leave Home Without It

Little items can add up to big expenses when you're traveling. If you get a headache or catch a cold, you can find yourself paying double or triple in a hotel lobby store for the basic medicines you need. As a result, it's a good idea to consider traveling with a small bottle of pain and fever reliever, Nyquil, and something to ease any stomach discomfort.

In order to avoid sickness while traveling, I've found it helpful to take echinacea and vitamin C a few days before, during, and after any trips—especially during the winter. In addition, I have purchased several boxes of antibacterial wipes. Every time I get on a new flight, I wipe down the armrests, tray table, and seat belt. It may sound silly, but I've seen a rapid decrease in the amount of times I've come home from a trip with a cold.

For sheer comfort, I always pack my own pillow from

home, and I like to bring along jasmine tea bags, favorite snacks, and room freshener or deodorizer to eliminate the musty smell from my hotel rooms. These little ways of treating myself nicely help me stay well rested and upbeat.

Even if you're only going away for the weekend, you should always pack an extra set of clothes in your carry-on bag. During one recent busy travel period, the airlines lost my luggage four trips in a row. While I'm still calculating the odds on anything like that happening again, I am humbled to admit that I only had fresh clothes with me one of the four times. I've also learned that it's a good idea to take a snapshot of your luggage and put it in your carry-on so that you can show the agent what the missing luggage looks like. If your luggage arrives broken, let an airline agent know right away. Don't leave the airport. Take the time to fill out the claim paperwork.

> **Give It!**
>
> It's a good idea to carry a stack of one-dollar bills with you when you travel for tipping everyone from shuttle drivers to housekeepers to concierges.

Sites to See—And Ways to Afford the Price of Admission

Whether you want to try to ski, tan on the beach, take in Alaska, or travel to Paris, the biggest key to affording the Ultimate Vacation is to travel off-season. Holidays are the most expensive time of the year at ski resorts, theme parks, beaches, and other popular vacation spots. Do your kids have good grades? Is it worth missing a few days of school to experience the trip they'll remember for a lifetime? Are you willing to take time away from work when it is not summertime? If the answer is yes, then you can choose, for example, to visit Disney World on a Tuesday in February when most of the rest of the world is in school and bargains are readily available. You'll find the experience much more pleasant when you can afford more for less, and you can enjoy what you are paying for without overwhelming crowds and lines.

If theme parks are the Ultimate Vacation for your family, Florida is the state where you can do it all. When planning a five-star theme park-oriented vacation, especially with children, carefully choose early on the lodgings that will best suit your needs. This is probably not the area where you want to be overly frugal, because the whole family will be residing in whatever type of hotel or time-share you choose. You may want an upscale hotel, which you can secure through Priceline, or you may want to try SkyAuction or other sites offering rental homes or time-share rentals.

With hotels, you'll get daily maid service, plus toiletries and other amenities. If you choose to stay in a Disney resort, the price can be higher, but you can coordinate rooms, theme park admissions, and even meal reservations all at one time. Guests staying in Disney resorts even get to enter the theme parks an hour earlier and stay later, in some cases, than regular visitors.

Keep in mind, however, that in a hotel you will probably be eating

Live It!

The best time to head to a major ski area is the last two weeks of January and the first week of February. Sandwiched between Martin Luther King Jr.'s birthday and President's weekend, you'll find the snow plentiful—especially if you're skiing out West—and less traffic on the slopes. Another option is to go skiing during the last two weeks of a ski area's season. Hotels and restaurants, and ski shops are trying to clear the merchandise to make room for next year's products. (Booking a trip for the end of the season always carries a risk that the snow will have melted or the conditions won't be as good, so take this into account as you make your reservations.)

Five-Star Fact

Invest in a good camera and videocamera and learn how to use them before taking your Ultimate Vacation. The photos and videos that you can look back at years later are often one of the best parts!

★ ★ ★ ★ ★

Five-Star Fact

If you want the experience of visiting an African savannah right from your hotel balcony, splurge on a stay at Disney's Animal Kingdom Lodge. The hotel is covered inside with African-themed art and the rooms are well appointed, but it is what's outside your window that makes it worth the minimum rates of $200 and up per night. The hotel has a 30-acre savannah with giraffes, impala, Thompson gazelles, zebra, wildebeest, and other African animals just a few hundred feet outside your balcony. Guests can also wander outside the lodge to the big campfire surrounded by rocking chairs, the 11,000-square-foot pool, or check out the animals through night goggles.

★ ★ ★ ★ ★

all of your meals out (due to the lack of a kitchen), tipping baggage handlers, and paying parking or valet fees.

If you want to stay in an economy-priced hotel but don't want to sacrifice quality, you will really need to do your homework. Popular vacation spot hotels such as in Orlando run the gamut from less-than-stellar to stupendous. Visit the hotel's website, but also search the Internet for hotel reviews and virtual tours. Ask friends and family members where they have stayed, and take advantage of any bargains they have found.

When deciding which theme parks you should visit and for how long, consider your investment and the quality of your vacation time you want to experience. Each theme park can take at least one full day to visit, and you need some downtime in between. If you want to do more than two or three parks, try to visit for at least a week. Before buying your tickets, look at all the options to get the best value. One-day tickets are rarely the best. Multiday tickets almost always offer additional value. Disney now offers "Magic Your Way" ticket pricing, allowing guests to choose the number of days and options they want to include, from "park hopping" (unlimited access to the four main parks) to water parks or DisneyQuest inclusion.

Orlando 14-day FlexTickets allow users unlimited access to Sea World, Universal Studios, Islands of Adventure, Wet-N-Wild, and Busch Gardens in Tampa for just over $200 at www.ticketmania.com. Compare that to the nearly $60 one-day, one-park admission price, and you can enjoy tremendous savings.

If you are a resident of a state where theme parks are located, consider buying an annual pass. Usually you can save money if you go as few as two times. Passes also often include special perks, such as discounted shopping in park stores, free parking, and admission to special events.

Of course, Orlando isn't the only place to visit theme parks. Southern California is home to Disneyland and the California Adventure, Knott's Berry Farm, and other attractions. Hershey Park, Pennsylvania, has a whole theme park built around its famous chocolate, there are more than two dozen theme parks across the United States owned by the Six Flags company, and that

Five-Star Fact

Orange Lake Country Club in Kissimmee and Bonnet Creek Resort are two of the nicest time-share facilities of the dozens my family has toured or tried. Orange Lake is four miles from the Disney parks, with beautiful villas situated on 1250 acres. The property includes eight pools, an 80-acre lake, water sports, court sports, seven restaurants, three pro shops, a theater, an Internet café, four championship golf courses, a 36-hole miniature golf course, daily activities, nightly entertainment, on-site ticket and transportation services, and a Disney Planning Center. Units range from studios to three-bedroom villas that rent anywhere from $500 to $2000 per week. Visit www.iVacation.com or do a search for "Orange Lake Country Club rentals" for more information. Bonnet Creek is the only lodging within the Disney gates that does not belong to Disney. (One man owned a piece of property in the middle of all the land purchased by the Disney Company and refused to sell to Disney. He even had it written into his will, and it is now owned by Fairfield Resorts.) It is absolutely gorgeous and is serviced by Disney transportation straight to the parks. Weekly rental units can be tough to come by but can be found at www.myresortnetwork.com for $795 (one bedroom) to $2300 (four bedrooms).

★ ★ ★ ★ ★

just scratches the surface. Custom-build your own theme park vacation, and do it the five-star way!

Tips for a Truly Five-Star Theme Park Experience

- Plan as much downtime as possible during the day and in between theme park visits so everyone stays upbeat.

- Bring disposable earplugs for use at loud concerts, during fireworks, or when rooming with snorers! Sleeping masks can be helpful too.

- Get lots of rest each night.

- Apply sunscreen liberally and frequently. Sunburn makes you absolutely miserable.

- Try to stock and drink plenty of bottled water.

- Bring disposable flashlights or reading lights so that bedtime reading or activities can be done in the same room with others who want to sleep.

- Encourage kids to put the video games, iPods, and CD players away. The vacation itself is plenty of stimulation, and you need time to interact as a family.

- Always pack disposable hooded ponchos (which can usually be found at dollar stores).

- Bring walkie-talkies or cell phones, and make sure to create a plan with your traveling companions in case someone gets lost.

- Prepare yourselves for waiting in long lines, especially if you travel during peak season.

- Get a map of the theme park ahead of time, and figure out which direction everyone wants to go so that you can cover all the most important bases for everyone.

- Save your souvenir purchases for the very end of

the day. Even small packages can become extremely heavy if you have to carry them all day. Also, thousands of items get dropped or left on the rides each year.

Cruises

Cruises are many people's idea of the Ultimate Vacation because you get to spend time on the ocean, visit exotic locations, and don't have to plan a thing. Food is available and included in the price of the cruise, and there are plenty of activities onboard. For the ultimate five-star cruise, again, the rule of thumb is off-season. Even just a few weeks before or after can save hundreds of dollars per person. Remember that different cruise destinations have different peak seasons, so do your homework.

For example, one of the best ways to see Alaska is by taking a cruise, with cruises through southeast Alaska scheduled from mid-May through mid-September. The May cruises are often called "shake down" cruises that allow the crew members and staff to get things running smoothly before the ship is at full capacity. That's why booking a cruise in mid-May can save you money. But the real reason to book a cruise early in the season is the weather. Some of the most beautiful and least rainy days of the year in southeast Alaska are in May.

Investigate what style of cruise and clientele the ships you are considering offer. Are they primarily for singles or seniors? Do they attract lots of families with young children? Also factor in the size of the ship. Smaller ships may be less

Five-Star Fact

Consider becoming a member of AAA. For around $100 to $150 a year, not only will AAA tow your car for free up to 100 miles if it breaks down (if you are a "plus" member), but also the association offers free trip planning, maps, and brochures, plus travel discounts and packages of all kinds. One little-known perk: Members can also get passport photos taken at any AAA office for free.

★ ★ ★ ★ ★

expensive, but those who experience seasickness will feel it more. Find out the age of the ship you want to sail on, the size, and what amenities it offers for the price. Cruises Only, *www.cruisesonly.com*, is a great site for searching through all the worldwide cruise lines and destinations for the five-star cruise for you.

When you find a deal that looks good, be sure to read all of the fine print so that you are not stuck paying additional port fees and taxes. Get quotes that include all fees. Port fees can run a couple hundred dollars per passenger. Remember that if you want to purchase cruise insurance, get it from an insurance company, not the agency booking your cruise. You will often get better coverage at a lower price. Cruise insurance should cover trip cancellation either by you or the cruise line, plus medical expenses and lost or damaged luggage.

Go for cabins with the size you need, not necessarily whether they are interior or have windows. Interior cabins are less expensive, and chances are you will not be spending much time in your cabin except when you have your eyes closed to sleep at night. Experts recommend bringing a clock or some way of telling time if you have an interior cabin, because no daylight comes into the room. Note that rates, like most travel packages, are usually based on double occupancy, or two people in the cabin. If you want to travel alone, you will pay a much higher "single" rate. On the flip side, if you want three or four in your cabin, make sure that all of you are not paying the full rate. The additional people should pay a reduced rate.

> ### Live It!
>
> To create a five-star vacation, make sure you take the weather in your vacation area into account before you travel. You may get rock-bottom prices at a particular destination because it has snowed in nine years out of ten on the dates you choose. Or the waters where you want to cruise are likely to be choppy due to storms at the height of hurricane season.

International Travel

Beyond the borders of the United States, many people visit the wilds of Africa, the many cultures and countries of Europe and Asia, and the Amazon of South America. International travel can expand your knowledge and understanding of the world like no other experience.

To achieve a five-star international travel experience, it is often advisable to go with an established tour to take in the most famous sites and provide the most convenience for the money. Tours get you there, provide your accommodations and some meals, and take you around with guides and interpreters, if needed, to famous museums, churches, castles, and other sites.

You'll need to budget for your passports, *www.travel.state.gov/passport*, and apply for them at least six to eight weeks before you are going to need them, or you will have to pay an additional fee to get them expedited to you (which still takes about two weeks). Consider whether you need to exchange currency and what the rates are so you'll know exactly what you can afford. Be sure to calculate the time zones traveled, and build in time when you get home to recuperate from all the flying, the unfamiliar foods, and the laundry you'll need to wash. Pay attention to the political climates

Five-Star Fact

of the countries you want to see, and check out the Centers for Disease Control and Prevention, *www.cdc.gov/travel,* to see what vaccinations, if any, are recommended before you go.

If you are a picky eater and are traveling to a foreign country, study enough of the language beforehand to know what some of your favorite dishes are called. Also, pack some of your favorite snacks to have in your room. Take along a photo of your family, friends, or pets to remind you of home, and be sure to bring your business cards to hand out to all your newfound friends. Research what items your destinations are famous for, so you can bring home the souvenirs you really want to keep and share. China, for example, has excellent prices on pearls. Switzerland is known worldwide for its watches and chocolate, while Paris is the fashion capital of the world.

If you want to strike out on your own, make sure you investigate the best quality options for the best price. In Europe, for example, should you rent a car or get a Eurail pass, *www.raileurope.com,* that entitles you to ride the high-speed trains from country to country? Which sites do you want to see the most? Which off-the-beaten-path treats can you add in to experience more local

Give It!

For international travel that provides five-star blessings, if not accommodations, sign up for a short-term missions trip or visit a third world country. There are many organizations that will put people to work all over the world distributing food, digging wells, building homes, teaching, and helping those in desperate need. Contact almost any local church to point you in the direction of a short-term trip.

flavor? Make sure you have accommodations that are in a safe area and that you do not wander anywhere that would put you in danger.

There are hundreds of thousands of Internet blogs, chat sites, and travel sites that can answer your travel questions for anywhere around the world—from what to pack to where to eat to the most efficient way to get through customs checks. Try downloading the international travel search engine software at *www.sidestep.com* for instant comparisons of deals offered around the world.

Live It!

If the Ultimate Vacation is not in your budget of time or finances right now, don't put off creating one at home. You can have an Ultimate Vacation in your own hometown by carving out a Saturday for visiting the local flea markets, museums, or sites that you've never seen. Get away to a bed-and-breakfast, or set up a "spa day" for each other or friends at home. Get out the creams, oils, nail polishes, massagers, and foot baths, and turn off the computers, cell phones, and telephones. Don't look at the clock, and do not clean anything or do any work. Just relax for a day with your favorite books or movies. Spend time in prayer, light some candles, and eat your favorite foods. You can always go back to being busy and disciplined the next day, but it's the Ultimate Vacation days that will make all that work worthwhile.

The World As Your Oyster

★ Make the Internet your best friend in searching for the best deals on travel.

★ Educate yourself on travel auction sites and online travel brokers, such as Expedia and Orbitz.

★ Think outside the box and expand your search from traditional hotel stays to time-shares, house rentals, and home exchanges.

★ Learn various airline policies and perks, and join their frequent flyer programs.

★ Pack over-the-counter medications and all the toiletries you'll need for your trip in your suitcase. Prepare a smaller version and one set of clothes for your carry-on bag.

★ Pack the little comforts that will make your stay a blast—from favorite magazines and candy bars to your favorite pillow.

★ Seek out coupons and discount cards from professional membership organizations, your place of employment, the Internet, and publications.

★ Make the time to travel off-season. You'll get much better rates for everything.

★ Visit places you have always wanted to see.

★ Create the most luxurious and unique travel experiences that you can, so you can remember them fondly for a lifetime.

★ Find out the requirements for international travel before you go to make sure you have all the bases covered.

★ Add the nostalgia factor for an Ultimate Vacation down memory lane.

★ Put together your own idea of the Ultimate Vacation, including off-the-beaten-path attractions.

★ Take lots of video and pictures to relive your vacation years later.

★ Have an Ultimate Vacation at home if you can't afford the time or money to get away.

Entering the High-Tech World

Our lives in America are defined by our gadgets. We constantly talk on cell phones, check e-mail from wherever we are, and block out those around us with our iPods and CD players. We enjoy espresso machines, bread makers, and vacuums that run by themselves. Yep, we love our technology, but it does not have to bankrupt us. We can have a five-star life with plenty of toys and still have time and money to share with others.

E-Shopping

I lived on a small island in Alaska with limited shopping options for nearly two years before I discovered that I had access to the world's biggest mall 24 hours a day. It's called eBay. With a few quick clicks, I could track down one-of-a-kind items from around the planet, pay for them online, and have them delivered to my front door.

Technology has transformed the way we shop. Instead of heading out to the mall, we can enjoy perusing thousands and even millions of products, gadgets, and gizmos from the comfort of our own home. And with a little extra postage, the item can be on our doorstep the next day.

As technology pushes forward at breakneck speeds, the bells and whistles found on portable electronic devices are constantly changing, catering to more specific needs. The mere assortment of products can be overwhelming and costly. Before you head off to the mall or go online to shop for computers, cellular phones, PDAs, cameras, or other high-tech devices, five-star savvy shoppers will ask themselves:

- What kind of product am I looking for?

- What are the features I can't live without?

- What extra features would I like to have if I can afford them?

- How much am I able to spend on the item?

- How soon will the technology I am buying today be obsolete?

- What kind of extended warranties are available for these high-dollar items?

- What is the return policy or manufacturer's warranty if I can't make it work?

- Do I know how to use this item?

- Do I really need it or do I want it simply because it is the latest trendy toy?

- Will the technology I am investing in give me a positive return in my work or home life, or will it just take time better spent elsewhere?

- What kind of ratings and reviews has the product received?

Those are some pretty basic questions that far too few people bother to ask themselves. As a result, they come home with $3000 computers that have all kinds of programs and features they will never use (when a $1000 purchase would have been fine) but that are missing the basics they need (which can cost hundreds of dollars extra). They pick up high-tech gadgets that look cool but are nothing more than a passing fancy that will be obsolete by the end of the year.

The bottom line? The five-star way to shop for electronics boils down to the following:

- Know exactly what you need.

- Buy only what you need.

- Make sure it's quality.

If you are looking to buy something electronic, it's always worthwhile to visit *www.froogle.com*, a shopping site launched by Google that searches multiple sites including eBay, Amazon.com, and others for the best deal. So if you're looking for a deal on your next camera, portable DVD player, or iPod, you can do a quick search and organize the listings in terms of price. It's also worth visiting sites like *www.overstock.com* and *www.jandr.com*. You'll be able to compare the price, model, and other details with the click of a button. If you're looking for a specific iPod, for example, simply type the product with quotes around it to focus on the model you want.

Give It!

Looking to get rid of some old computer equipment? Check out the Computer for Schools Association (*www.pcsforschools.org*), which takes the equipment you donate and refurbishes it for use at schools, correctional facilities, and nonprofit organizations. Depending on your location, pickups can be arranged. Make it your personal policy that every time a new gadget comes in, an old one goes out to someone who needs it.

Computers

Investing in a computer system or laptop can be a scary proposition. What are all those "megs" and "rams," and who knows what the difference is between a Pentium and all the rest anyway? To techno-savvy computer folks, every one of those details is crucial, and they can tell you why. In fact, they usually love to let you know. Almost everyone knows someone who is a computer technician, programmer, or self-proclaimed computer geek. So when you want a five-star computer and you need to go shopping, take them with you. At the very least, call them before you go to the cash register and describe the computer you are considering. They can give you the right questions to ask, tell you what the computer can do for you, and let you know if you are paying too much. They may even suggest an online store where you can buy the best computer systems, parts, and upgrades.

Always consider your needs and space. Do you want a flat screen, a DVD player that also records, or great software to do video editing or animation? Would it be wise to invest in a PC, or will a laptop do the trick because you are on the road a lot?

Warranties

The extended warranty for a PC or laptop can run up to $299 for three years; however, just one repair can make it pay for itself. Also, the warranty should cover the laptop battery, so near the end of your warranty period you can turn your battery in to get a new one if needed at about half the cost of the policy alone. Best Buy's extended warranties cover everything from vacuums to portable CD players to Game Boys. For some items that have a manufacturer's defect, Best Buy will issue you a credit for the original price paid, which means you can often get an updated replacement for the same price or less, since technology changes so rapidly.

For example, I purchased a Compaq Ipaq PDA a couple of years ago, and I had it nearly a year before the screen began shorting out repeatedly. The internal spring mechanism was also faulty and would not hold the stylus in place. By the time I returned it under my extended warranty, the Ipaq had been upgraded several times. I paid $400 for the original unit, and the current faster, better ones with more memory and features were only $300. Under my extended warranty I got a brand-new PDA and a $100 credit to spend on something else. The price I paid for that extended warranty? Sixty dollars. The peace of mind I get by knowing my electronics will be fixed or replaced when I need them? Priceless.

> **Live It!**
>
> As you are sifting through your high-tech options, always ask about extended warranties. They can be lifesavers for computers and other electronic items. Best Buy offers one of the top extended warranty policies I've seen. Not only do they provide in-home service for PCs so you don't have to unplug all the cords and cables to carry your computer into the store and then leave it for weeks, but also they have a "No Lemon" policy that will replace your unit if it has had to be repaired more than three times. (Certain things are excluded, like intentional damage, of course.)

Sam's Club, Circuit City, and other stores also offer extended warranties. Just check the fine print to see what the policy includes before you buy. Generally, an extended warranty should offer two to four years for no more than 25 percent of what the item cost you.

For household appliances, extended warranties can also save you a bundle. While there are some companies that cover your entire household one year at a time, others like GE and Sears bundle appliances together for one, two, three, or five years or offer single-appliance policies. Also, the company offering the warranty does not necessarily have to be the same "brand" as the appliance itself. For example, a Sears warranty might cover a GE appliance, and vice versa. Check the policy details to be sure. If you cannot afford to replace an older washer or dryer right away and it can be covered for all parts and labor for a year for under a hundred dollars, it may be worth the investment. Like all "insurance," you may never need it. But it sure is nice when you do and it is there.

Connecting to the Net

Depending on how much time you're online, it's worth upgrading from a basic dial-up service to cable modem or DSL. Based on your area, you'll spend two or three times as much to be online, but you'll save a tremendous amount of time and enjoy the benefits of high-speed service. With dial-up service, sending or receiving a photo can stall your connection for several minutes, while a high-speed connection can send or receive the same image in a matter of seconds.

Check with the cable company in your area if you want to go with cable modem service. The Internet connection comes in through the shared cable network, which the company runs to your home if you don't already have cable. When you wait for their specials, they will usually install the cable free and give you the cable modem. You will need to have an Ethernet card in your PC, but if you have a newer computer, it is probably already in there. (If not, they can be purchased for under $20.) Cable modem has a larger, faster broadband width but can be slowed down if many users are on at once. DSL runs through single phone lines but not through the portion you use for your calls, eliminating any privacy issues but not always as fast as cable. Wi-Fi is wireless Internet connections beamed

Live It!

One thing to note when buying any electronic item: Don't be in a hurry to throw the original packaging away for that PDA, cell phone, camera, videocamera, or computer. Many products need to be returned in their original boxes. So make a place in the attic, basement, or closet for those empty boxes, packing materials, extra cords or accessories, and instruction booklets. Many stores (including Best Buy) charge a hefty "restocking fee" if the returned items are not with the original accessories and packaging.

from satellites. It provides the most portable Internet access, although, as with cell phones, coverage is not available in all areas.

Cable connection or DSL should cost you somewhere between $25 and $75 per month for residential service. Business plans cost more. Look for sign-up specials, and take advantage of any savings the company might offer if you refer other customers.

T-Mobile is developing the largest visible number of Wi-Fi "hotspots" in the country, providing access to the Internet for a fee from most Starbucks locations and many airports. The service can be purchased hourly, daily, or monthly for use in any T-Mobile HotSpots. Visit *www.tmobile.com/hotspot* for coverage maps and pricing plans. Hotels and other public locations are also offering pay-as-you-use wireless connections offered by a variety of companies.

Phone Home

Even if you're not a chatty Cathy, you should still be looking for a good deal on your phone rates. Why? Because a five-star life is full of rewarding relationships. Having a low-cost phone plan will help give you the extra incentive

Live It!

After you have had Internet service for six months or more and you see better offers from your company being advertised to new customers, call the company and ask what kind of special or deal they will offer you to retain you as a customer. They know there are many other options available to you and will often give you a price break for the next 90 days or some other special. This also works with cellular phone companies and cable or satellite television providers.

Five-Star Fact

As of this writing, Panera restaurants nationwide offer free wireless in their restaurants. They also have great bread, soup, bakery items, and sandwiches. So you can have your Internet and eat there too. You can also find a comprehensive listing of wireless hotspots (free and fee-based) around the country at *www.jwire.com*. Check it before you go on your next trip, and you will find places to plug in and log on that don't cost you a penny.

★ ★ ★ ★ ★

you need to keep in touch with friends and family around the country.

When it comes to basic phone service, it's worth shopping around. Flip open your local yellow pages to find what companies are available. Even if you have had your service for several years, it's worth revisiting the issue of your local and long-distance carrier. When you call these companies, ask them about their basic rate and package plans. You may be able to tag on extra savings on features such as voice mail and call-waiting, but be careful about paying for too many bells and whistles, such as three-way calling, that you may not use very often. And be sure to ask about extra taxes and fees. One company may offer you a better initial rate, but by the time you tag on all the excess charges, you may be better off going with another company. Whatever company you decide is right, you'll need to review your bill carefully. Always check for questionable charges or services you didn't sign up for.

Give It!

Not sure what to do with your old cell phone? Consider donating it to Donate a Phone Call to Protect, an organization which fights against domestic violence by distributing reprogrammed phones with emergency numbers. For more information about this organization and others that can use your used cell phones, visit *www.wirelessfoundation.org.*

Regarding long distance, you may want to opt for a monthly plan that allows you a certain amount or unlimited minutes, but the best deals on long distance are usually found on calling cards purchased from warehouse stores such as Costco or Sam's Club. You can find cards that offer better price-per-minute rates, but many of these charge a minimum fee for every call placed. Whether they're tagging on a ten-minute penalty or 50¢ fee, you're better off looking for a card that only charges you for the time you use. With Costco and Sam's Club cards, for under four cents a minute you can call anywhere in the United States. The cards also feature great rates for calling internationally, and they can be used around the world—just be sure to bring the access number for the country you're calling from. Calling cards save you extra money because you can avoid many of the extra taxes and fees you'll pay even with the same rate on your home phone, and they're rechargeable.

Live It!

To avoid the excess charges accompanied with dialing 411, use the Internet to track down phone numbers. A quick visit to *www.yellowpages. com*, *www.whitepages.com*, *www. switchboard.com*, or *www.anywho. com* will save you some money. If you're trying to find an 800 number, call (800) 555-1212. It's a free listing of 800 numbers around the country.

Another high-tech option to save on long distance is using VoIP (Voice over Internet Protocol), which allows you to route your calls over the Internet. Similar to e-mail, VoIP allows you to call anywhere in the world for the same cost, so the savings on international calls is tremendous. VoIP has been around for years, but the growing number of broadband and high-speed Internet users have made it more commonplace. One of the best VoIP services is through Skype (*www.skype.net*), which allows you to download software called Softphone and enables you to call two dozen countries for a couple of cents a minute. Other companies, including AT&T, Vonage, and Verizon, also offer VoIP plans.

If you are online but don't want to use VoIP, then you should definitely maximize your access to e-mail and Instant Messaging to keep up with people you love. A variety of sites, including *www.yahoo.com* and *www.hotmail.com,* offer free e-mail. And some instant messengers, such as MSN, allow you to use your computer's microphone and speakers like a speakerphone.

If you have cable modem or DSL, you may not need to sign up for a local landline at all. Many people are choosing to go with cell phones instead. The best cell phone company and deal is going to be based on where you live in the country. Obviously, if you're in a metropolitan area you are going to have a lot more options than if you are in a rural one. Before you choose a cell company, talk to friends in your area. Ask about their cell service. What are the limitations of the coverage? How many calls are dropped? Have they had any billing problems? Also take time to look at the big picture of your life before signing up for a plan. Do you have friends and family you talk to a lot? Would joining the same cell service help cut your bill? Do you travel a lot and need a plan with unlimited roaming or coverage? And how many minutes do you actually need?

If you want to avoid the big fees associated with using more than your monthly allotment of minutes, consider using Minute Guard, *www.minute-guard.com*, which will send a text message or e-mail to remind you when you're running out of minutes. For less than $20 a year, you can literally save hundreds on your cell phone bill if you're a heavy user.

All Things Music

Music is everywhere these days, as people take their favorite songs with them wherever they go thanks to a little gadget called the iPod and the ability of computers to turn music into portable files called MP3s. CD players are also still in demand, MP3 players can make exercising with headphones on a cinch, and satellite radio means you can take your favorite radio stations with you without any decrease in signal from coast to coast. Nifty, huh?

XM and Sirius are the two main competitors for satellite radio service. Both offer more than 100 channels of music for less than $15 a month. Special satellite radio receivers must also be purchased, but they now make ones that can be transferred from car to home. You can find out more at *www.sirius.com* or *www.xmradio.com* for more information and rate plans.

To get the best sound from your radio, you need a good stereo system. But which one is right for you? Again, consult the experts. Visit a car stereo shop if you don't know anyone who is knowledgeable about brands and prices. Car stereo buffs usually know about all things audio and can point you in the right direction for home or car. When installing a new car stereo system, wait for the specials that offer free installation when you purchase the system from that particular store. For home theater sound, figure out how big the room is where you will be installing it so you can tell that to the salesman. No matter how many watts or amps it has, if you can't turn it up past a certain point without making art fall off the walls, the extra power is a waste.

Five-Star Fact

Bose offers great quality, but it's nearly impossible to find on sale. While eBay and other auction sites are an option, you should also consider sites like *www.sharperimage.com* and others that offer airline miles and even an occasional one-time discount. Other high-end speaker brands to look for include Cerwin-Vega and JBL.

★ ★ ★ ★ ★

Turning on the Television

Shopping for a television has become increasingly complex with the variety of models available. If you're thinking about buying a new television, below are a few factors to consider:

What role do you want television to play in your life? If you want to spend less time watching TV, then you may want to consider buying a smaller screen or placing the television someplace other than in your living room.

The size of your room and vehicle. Believe it or not, many people don't bother to measure the space available for the TV and bring it home only to discover that it doesn't fit at all. Some people find they don't have room in their car to transport it back to their home and have to hire a mover or borrow a vehicle from a friend.

The quality of the picture. Televisions use different display systems, and the best way to tell which one is best for you is by visiting a store where you can see the screens side by side. Which one is clearest? Does the picture seem grainy, or is there a greenish tint to it? Does the picture look particularly bright or flat? Does it deliver the detail and clarity you're looking for?

The quality of the sound. Just as the picture varies from model to model, the quality of the sound also varies among televisions. After you find the right television according to the screen, ask the salesman to turn up the volume and compare it to other models. Does it sound clear, harsh, or garbled?

The quality of the remote control. When you're in the store, the remote control may not seem like a priority, but once you bring it home it will be. Look at the features on the remote. Are they easy to use? Do they contain the features you regularly use?

What do reviewers say about the product? It's worth taking a look at back issues of *Consumer Reports, www.consumer reports.org,* to find out which models work the best.

Say "Cheese"!

Finding the right camera has become an increasingly important decision for people who want to record, document, and scrapbook every important moment of their five-star lives. Before you can capture that memory without red-eye or blurriness, you need to choose the right photography and video equipment.

When choosing a camera, it's important to consider whether you will be taking most of your shots inside or outside, whether you will be shooting moving subjects (such as professional sports players or small children running about), whether you want to just point and shoot and have pretty decent pictures with only a little time invested in the learning process, or whether you want to invest in learning how to do close-ups, portrait photography, low-light photography, and other special techniques requiring optional wide lenses, stronger flash equipment, and more manual settings.

For now, you can still choose between 35mm and digital cameras, although products are increasingly (and quickly) going digital. Digital photography can make even the worst photographer appear to be a pro with the help of some manipulation software, such as Photo Paint and Adobe, which will allow you to easily crop, paint, sharpen, and even change the lighting on all of your favorite digital photographs. You can zoom to a closeness of one inch with the zoom technology available to the digital world.

To view the photographs, there is also an immediate still photo left in the viewfinder/video screen on the camera itself, enabling the photographer to see if anyone had his eyes closed or the picture came out blurry. Digital prints can be put on a CD or printed at home or in-store. One of the current disadvantages to digital cameras is their flash capacity. The cost of printing at home, when you factor in the photo paper and the ink required, is a little higher, but the difference is negligible.

If you are a decent photographer and want the sharpest clarity and best quality pictures, you can still stick—for now—with your 35 mm. Check with *Consumer Reports* for the best brands and prices of both kinds of cameras.

Gizmos and Gadgets

Household appliances have also gone high-tech, with robotic vacuums that float around rooms by themselves and fancy coffee "pod" machines that brew a single perfect cup. If electronic items are your favorite thing, visit *www.woot.com* for a special treat. Each day they post limited quantities of one product at an incredible deal. Recent products included a 12-cup Cuisinart coffee maker for $39.99 and an Early Warning Radar and Laser detector for $42.99 (plus $5 shipping and handling). Woot.com is like a daily treasure hunt—you never know what you'll find. Products can sell out quickly, so it's generally better to view items in the mornings.

Another suggestion is to visit *www.propertyroom.com*. This website is run by Property Bureau, a California company that uses the site to sell items from the property rooms of 425 police and sheriff's departments in 30 states. You can find all kinds of items up for auction, including computers, stereos, and various electronics, at bargain-basement prices. Recent auctions items included a Canon EOS Elan II SLR Camera with flash attachment, a blue canvas bag, lens cleaning tissues, and other accessories. With one day left, the bidding stood at $250. Other items ranged from an 1887-O Morgan silver dollar to a Mongoose EFX boy's bicycle. Item descriptions are fairly thorough, including a rating of the condition of the item. Take shipping into account before you bid. Items must be shipped Federal Express (ground or express), or the items can be picked up at their various locations.

Five-Star Fact

You can save big on new and refurbished kitchen gadgets at *www.kitchencollection.com,* where you'll find items such as a KitchenAid's five-quart mixer in like-new condition for nearly half the original price.

★ ★ ★ ★ ★

For gadgets that make life simpler, remember that a five-star life is not a cluttered one. Small kitchen appliances of all shapes and sizes can be cool, but the oven, the microwave, and a good coffeemaker will go a long way to making your life happy. If you want ice-cream makers, donut fryers, sandwich pressers, espresso machines, bread makers, cotton candy machines, juicers, and other individual appliances, you need somewhere to put them. If your kitchen is not designed for great storage—where you can see and get to your gadgets easily—chances are they will get put away to collect dust. If you want to have a variety of small appliances and they must sit on the kitchen counters, invest in items that look good, so that your kitchen can have a uniform design that is pleasing. After all, you will have to look at them several times a day!

Choose household electronics with an eye for durability and efficiency. You want machines that do the most for you with the least effort expended. If you have to hook all kinds of belts and hoses together every time you want to use your canister vacuum, you may not use the appliance as much as you should. On the other hand, if you invest in a quality robotic room vacuum, it will clean the room by itself, freeing you up for other things!

Five-Star Fact

Roomba, the robotic floor vacuum, propels itself around any flat surface, picking up dust, pet hair, and other items. This machine works like a spiraling pool cleaner and could be great for tile and hardwood floors and has a charging/docking station and/or batteries. It ranges from $150 to $300 on various websites. Check out *www.biz rate.com* for a comparison of current deals.

★ ★ ★ ★ ★

Action Points

Entering the High-Tech World

★ Be true to your techno self. Know exactly what you need and what it should cost before you go shopping.

★ Consider using calling cards over a traditional long-distance service at home.

★ Find out if a cell phone would save you more than a land-line.

★ Upgrade from dial-up to cable modem or DSL if you use e-mail or the Internet on a regular basis.

★ Take advantage of the free wireless hotspots when you need Internet on-the-go.

★ Give your old, working electronic equipment to those in need.

★ Compare the visual and audio features of televisions before you buy.

★ Consider purchasing an extended warranty for any electronic item.

★ Keep the original packaging of all electronic items during the warranty period to avoid restocking fees if the item must be returned.

★ Buy the equipment that will save you time.

Big-Ticket
Items

For most of us, the vast majority of our purchases are under $1000, but every so often we are going to make a significant purchase. Whether it's a home, furniture, or a car, five-star bargain hunters take the time to become savvy shoppers before they shell out the big bucks. It's important to learn how to make the most of your money and your purchases—big and small.

Home Sweet Home

If you are thinking about purchasing a home in the near future, then you need to determine what you can afford. The general rule of thumb is that your maximum purchase price should be no more than two- to two-and-a-half times your annual gross income depending on mortgage interest rates. With those figures in mind, if interest rates are lower, you are going to be able to buy a more expensive piece of property than when interest rates are higher. A variety of websites, including *www.us.hsbc.com*, provide online calculators to help you determine what you can afford. It's important to remember that on top of your principle and interest payment, you will have to factor in closing costs, which total between two to five percent of your loan. You'll also have to tag on taxes and insurance, which can boost the total of your mortgage by 30 percent or more. So if your total mortgage payment is $1000 a month, odds are that almost one third of that is going to property taxes and homeowner's insurance.

Live It!

One general rule of thumb when figuring out what house you can afford is that your housing costs should fall between 18 and 24 percent of your net monthly income.

When you start looking for a home, take into consideration the value and condition of the surrounding houses and neighborhoods. Are property values in the area going up or down? Does the home include acreage or sit on a lot? Is the community deed-restricted, and what are the annual home owner association fees? If you are buying a condominium, make sure to find out if it is restricted to seniors, excludes pets, or includes high maintenance fees that can make your monthly payment outrageous.

Another thought to keep in mind is to resist the urge to impulse buy when you look at a home. Impulse buying a lipstick might set you back $10. Impulse buying a home that really doesn't fit your needs can set you back 30 years of mortgage payments, stress, and frustration. Make a list of the criteria that will fit your needs, including whether you want to live in the country or city, the necessary number of bedrooms and bathrooms, how much square footage you need, and the lot size or acreage. Figure out which school the neighborhood is zoned for, and drive around to see what's nearby. If you count on having a Target in your backyard and the nearest one is an hour away, you may want to look at another house.

When our family wanted to move to a bigger home, we searched for two years but were unable to find a house that met our specific criteria for under a half million dollars in our county. We had to decide whether to lower our expectations, increase what we would pay, or expand our search geographically. We decided to look at the counties around us and searched newspaper ads and real estate websites. One Sunday we drove through four counties, checking off a list of 10 to 20 properties that looked promising on paper and online but didn't measure up when we visited. At ten o'clock that evening, with three kids asleep in the van, we started to head for home when we decided to go ahead and drive by the last house on the list. It was slightly smaller than we had agreed we wanted, but it looked really nice online.

From the moment we drove into the beautiful estate community, we knew it was different than anything else we had seen that day. Pulling up to the brand-new designer house that was for sale, we were so excited that we crept up to the windows and peered in. We called the Realtor the next morning, and she showed us the house the following day. We decided on an offer as well as the top price we were willing to pay. The seller countered our first offer, but by the end of the week we had a deal. We had to move our family about 50 miles from our previous home, but it was one of the wisest decisions we

Give It!

Each year for more than a decade, the St. Jude Children's Research Hospital has teamed up with builders, landscape designers, interior decorators, and furniture companies to construct homes valued between $200,000 and $500,000 throughout the country to be raffled off in support of St. Jude's. Participants can purchase tickets at $100 each for a chance to win these homes in many cities, along with other valuable prizes. A maximum of 10,000 tickets is sold for each Dream Home Giveaway, raising a potential $1 million in each participating city each year. St. Jude Children's Research Hospital treats pediatric patients of catastrophic diseases, mostly cancer, and researches those diseases to discover new treatments and cures. The best part? Families never pay for any treatment not covered by insurance. Visit *www.stjude.org/dreamhome* for more information.

ever made. It turns out that we had moved into a county that was ranked the fastest-growing in the state, and as a result our home nearly doubled in value in the first two years.

Once you have a ballpark figure of what you can afford in a given area, it's worth visiting a mortgage broker to find out exactly what you can borrow. Otherwise, you may begin looking at homes and fall in love with something that's out of reach. Don't set yourself up for heartbreak.

Keep in mind that a mortgage company or real estate agent isn't going to tell you what you're going to be able to afford. They are going to tell you how much an institution will loan you. There is a big difference. You may be able to borrow a quarter of a million dollars, but the stress required to stretch your dollars each month to pay the mortgage and escrow the taxes may be more than you can bear. Only you can figure out what you can comfortably handle, especially with plans for the future that may include travel, children, or retirement. Five-star buyers do not allow themselves to buy more home than they can afford. That is one of the quickest ways to lower your overall quality of life.

While some mortgage companies allow you to buy homes with little or no money down, you'll be best off putting down the largest percentage of the purchase price you can. Not only can you avoid PMI (private mortgage insurance), but also you will have lower mortgage payments for the entire duration of your loan.

When shopping for a home, you need to look for a trustworthy, reputable, and well-seasoned real estate agent. The simplest of real estate transactions can become complex fast, and you want someone who is honest, educated, and working for your best interests. Talk to people you know about the real estate agent they used. Remember that some agents pay referral fees, so don't rely on just one recommendation. Once you find an agent you are interested in working with, find out how long they have been licensed and lived in the area.

If it's just a few years, you may want to consider going with a more experienced agent.

Depending on the demand for homes in your area, you may or may not be able to negotiate the sale price. Once you have agreed on a price with the seller, it's time to secure a mortgage. This is an area where a few price comparisons and a little hard work can add up to thousands of dollars in savings. Most mortgage brokers are highly competitive. They will do whatever they can to get your business.

When my husband and I recently purchased our first home in Alaska, I visited a mortgage broker who had been recommended by a friend. She offered us several rates based on adjustable or fixed mortgage rates and provided a good faith estimate, which included the interest rate and all the fees associated with the loan. I took the estimate to the mortgage broker across the street, and she immediately knocked the origination fee of nearly $2000 off the loan. Then I took the revised good faith estimate to a third mortgage broker. Again, he was able

Live It!

10 Golden Rules of Real Estate:

1. Location. Location. Location. It's better to buy a smaller home in a desirable area of town than a large home in an area of town that no one wants (or will want).

2. In a specific neighborhood, it's generally better to own a smaller home instead of the largest when it comes to resale.

3. Always ask about the electric and other utility bills. Factor the energy efficiency of your home into the purchase.

4. Remember that highly unique or one-of-a-kind homes can be difficult to sell.

5. Always have a qualified engineer inspect the home before you make a purchase.

6. Visit the house you're considering buying at different times of the day. Traffic, construction, and nearby activities may create more noise than you anticipated.

7. Always take into account the general area when making a home purchase. Find out about school systems, shopping, pollution, and safety in the area.

8. Consider resale when you buy a home. Features such as a garage, paved driveway, ratio of bedrooms and bathrooms, and age of the appliances should be kept in mind in order to maximize your investment.

9. Before you close on your home, ask the seller to include a home warranty for one or more years, or ask your real estate agent to exempt a portion of his fees so you can buy one. Warranties can save you headaches in the first year if the appliances quit, the pool leaks, or the air-conditioning goes out.

10. Remember that real estate agents work on commission, and their percentages are negotiable. Some agents are willing to take less to negotiate the deal. All you have to do is ask. The worst they can say is no.

to knock the mortgage costs down by a few hundred dollars. Finally, I took this mortgage broker's good faith estimate back to the first mortgage broker. She was able to match all of the previous offers and found a lower interest rate because of my husband's employer. In the end, two afternoons of bouncing between mortgage brokers saved more than $5000 in interest and expenses associated with the loan.

Live It!

ARM versus Fixed Rate

When it comes to mortgages, you'll have to choose between an adjustable and a fixed rate mortgage.

An *ARM (adjustable rate mortgage)* has an interest rate that changes after a certain amount of time, usually between three and ten years.

A *fixed rate mortgage* keeps the same payment for the entire length of the loan, which is usually 15 or 30 years.

You should talk to a financial advisor about which option is best for you.

Once you have a contract on a house and have found the right mortgage company, you will be asked to secure home insurance. Again, this is an area where a few phone calls can save you hundreds of dollars a year. I called six different local insurance companies, many of which represented national carriers. Prices varied widely. One name-brand company quoted an annual insurance rate of more than $1100, while the one we settled on was a mere $350 for the same coverage. The reason for the wide disparity is that a handful of companies base the cost on your credit rating. Thus, a good credit rating can dramatically decrease your home insurance costs.

Even if you have owned a home and had the same insurance policy for several years, it may be worth your time to shop around and price a new home owner's policy. It only requires a few phone calls, and you may find hundreds of dollars in savings.

After you close on your home, it will be time to pay your first mortgage payment. Whether you settled on a 15-year or 30-year loan or chose an adjustable mortgage rate, it pays off big-time to put any extra money you can toward your prin-ciple (the amount you owe). Paying one extra mortgage pay-ment per year can knock years off the life of your loan. Even an extra $20 or $50 a month can help reduce the overall number of payments you have to make.

Furnishing Your Home

After you jump through the hoops to buy a home, it's time to furnish it. While all those college wares of milk crates and futons worked while you were getting a degree, you'll probably want to upgrade your decor.

When it comes to furnishing a home, you need to con-sider where you want to spend your money. If meals are ex-tremely important to you, then you should consider investing in a quality dining room table. If you spend a lot of time in the living room, then you may want to put your money into higher quality couches. Think about what room of the house is the most important and focus a larger percentage of your budget in that area.

For example, my home has one large great room which combines the kitchen, living room, and dining room. My husband and I love sitting together at the end of a long day. We chose to spend several thousand dollars on the new couch, love seat, and armchair with an ottoman that seemed perfect for us. We were willing to cut back in other areas for the comfort of the couch set. To meet our budget, we purchased a large mission-size table and six chairs from an ad in the newspaper for $500. We purchased accent pieces for the room, including a coffee table and desk lamp from IKEA (*www.ikea.com*). By choosing to spend more in some areas and less in others, we were able to create a comfort-able, homey atmosphere we enjoy and still managed to stay under budget.

While great deals on furniture can be found through newspaper ads, flyers, and word of mouth, another option is going online. Craig's List, *www.craigslist.com*, connects buyers and sellers in a given region. You can find all kinds of secondhand furniture, sporting equipment, and appliances. Available in cities around the country, Craig's List offers users the benefit of connecting with other local users to actually see the item before you buy.

Purchasing a Car

Sooner or later you're going to need a new set of wheels. While a Ferrari may not be in your budget, you can still enjoy the comfort, ease, and reliability of a more economically sound ride.

When it comes to reviewing cars, *Consumer Reports* is a good guide. Their annual review of automobiles highlights the strengths and weaknesses of a variety of models. A quick visit to the library will allow you to research cars from earlier years and review them. A second indispensable guide is *Kelley Blue Book, www.kbb.com,* which will allow you to see the blue book value of a given automobile and know the value of your own vehicles.

Give It!

Whenever you upgrade a piece of furniture with something new, consider donating the older piece to charity. Lots of families could use your extra pieces.

Edmunds.com has developed its own resource for car buyers called *True Market Value* (TMV) pricing. The pricing system is based on actual sales figures derived from the average price that buyers are paying for a vehicle in your area. It's a handy reference when you're pricing a vehicle. It's also important to talk to friends and family who own a car similar to the one you want to buy. Every car has its own personality and quirks, and you may discover that there are engineering or design issues that you don't want to live with.

Buying New

If your standard of Five-Star Living is to own a new car, then you need to realize that the moment you drive the car off of the lot it immediately loses 20 percent of its value and becomes a used vehicle. If you want to buy a new car, wait until end-of-the-year sales when dealerships need to clear their lots. Those wanting to experience true Five-Star Living wait to buy the model they want when it is about two years old for maximum value at minimum price.

Before you ever step onto a car dealership lot, you need to do your research. Find out which features are standard in the car you want to purchase. Learn as much about the car as you can. Then, when you're talking to a dealer, you can sprinkle your knowledge into the conversation to let the salesperson know you've done your home-work.

Once you arrive at the dealership, take your time. Don't appear too eager or aggressive to make a purchase. If you don't have to have the exact car that moment, it's better to wait a day or two before you purchase. Always remember that the salespeople may be using manipulative or high-pressure tactics on you.

Janella, a single 29-year-old, recently visited a new car dealership to buy her very first new car. She was approached by a super friendly salesman who invited her to test drive the vehicle she really wanted. She loved the car! The salesman invited her into the dealership to talk to his manager about a possible deal. The salesman and his manager then teamed up to use the "good cop/bad cop" technique. The salesman acted as the good cop, asking Janella to make an offer on the car; and the manager acted as the bad cop to negotiate the deal.

Janella was savvy enough to know that she should not make the first offer but should tell the salesman that she needed to know his lowest price. The salesman disappeared to talk to his manager. The price he returned with was more than Janella wanted or planned to pay. That's when the haggling began. After several rounds, it was clear she would not be able to get close to the price she could afford. Rather than make an impulse buy, she wisely told the salesman she was going home to think about it.

Dealerships do not want potential customers to leave, knowing that the odds are good that they will not return. The salesman spoke once more with his manager, and the manager tried to get Janella to buy the car by blaming her failure to close the deal on his salesman and threatening to fire him.

Janella recognized this as a vulgar case of manipulation and left the dealership. A few weeks later she found the same car she originally wanted for more than $1000 less at another dealership. Five-star shoppers do not let manipulative sales tactics intimidate them into doing anything they will regret.

Let the Shopping Begin

Once you've begun looking at new cars, it's important to take note of the manufacturer's standard retail price (MSRP), and rest assured that the price tag on the windshield is highly negotiable. Instead of looking at the MSRP, ask the dealer to show you the manufacturer's invoice. To find out what the car is really selling for, consider visiting *www.fightingchance.com*, a company which serves as an information boutique for car shoppers. For a fee, the company will give you the latest pricing on new vehicles, so you know the true price before you make an offer.

A dealership naturally wants to move as many cars as possible, so they want your business. There are certain situations that give you an advantage over the dealership. For example, if a car has been on their lot for six to nine months, the dealership is in a position where they need to move the car so they can make room for one that will sell more quickly. Also, remember that salespeople often have a quota of sales or rewards for selling a certain amount in a given time period. That's why shopping at the end of the month or end of the year can yield better bargains. It's also important to note the time of year. Four-wheel-drive vehicles are naturally going to be reduced during the summer months, and sporty convertibles will be a better value during the winter. Visit multiple car dealerships too. Prices can vary widely.

> **Live It!**
>
> If you're going to be a five-star car shopper, then you're going to have to do your homework. Remember that an automobile qualifies as a major purchase, so take your time and choose carefully.

Some dealerships are willing to take trade-ins. The upside of trading in your car is that you save time and energy by changing cars in a single transaction. The downside of trading in your car is that it's hard to get its full value from the dealership. In addition, the salesman may artificially inflate the value of your new vehicle so that you feel like you're getting a better deal than you really are.

You'll also want to take advantage of any rebates or incentives. It's worth a visit to *www.edmunds.com* to check out the latest discounts from automakers, but be aware that some of the deals are limited to specific regions of the country. You may also find that taxes on automobiles vary widely between states, so if you live in a border town it may be worth your while to purchase the vehicle in a different state and then register it in your own if the laws allow.

Before you sign the final papers, you may want to make a quick call to your insurance agent or get a quick quote from *www.geico.com* or *www.progressive.com*. You just might be surprised at the price difference of insurance between different years, makes, and models.

Used Cars

Used cars today are more reliable than ever before, and many of them are still under warranty through the dealership or outside warranty companies. That means you can enjoy the benefits of a new car for a significantly lower cost. Not only will you save on insurance by buying a used car, but you'll also be able to use the money you saved to invest in something that will grow in value rather than decrease. Buying a used car means that you can buy a better car for less, which is exactly what Five-Star Living is all about.

Five-Star Quote

"[It's] kind of a silent protest at work—I just don't understand why I have to prove to people that I make money."

—*Topher Grace,*
on his seen-better-days
black Volkswagen Jetta

★ ★ ★ ★ ★

If you're looking for a newer used car, one option is to consider buying your vehicle from a car rental company. Many of the major brands turn over their fleet every one to two years, and you can enjoy a clean, well-maintained vehicle. The rental car company has already absorbed the majority of depreciation that comes in the first year of owning the car. Be cautious about the wear and tear on rental cars, which may have been driven hard—accumulating many miles in a very short period of time. Before buying, have any used car thoroughly checked out by a mechanic you trust. If you know any attorneys who handle personal estates, cars are often liquidated from estates and may be offered for a price that is under market value. Local credit unions can be a good source for used vehicles because they often liquidate repossessed vehicles.

Another option is to go online. One of our friends, Dave, was scanning through some sale items on eBay, and he decided on a whim to visit the auto section. He found a four-wheel-drive Lexus perfect for his wife, and ended up buying the car at a great price. Along the way, he learned some lessons that apply to anyone who is shopping for a car online—whether you're using *www.ebaymotors.com* or *www.autotrader.com:*

- Read all feedback and ratings regarding the seller.

- Ask for lots of photos of the vehicle. Dave says that there were more than 30 digital photos of the Lexus' outside and interior available online—so he knew what he was getting.

- Talk to the seller. Don't be afraid to ask questions about the car, such as where it came from, and about the seller's history with selling cars online.

> **Live It!**
> Always check the vehicle's history using the 17-digit VIN number at sites such as *www.carfax.com*. You'll be able to find out if the car was in an accident, submerged in water, or stolen.

- Do your homework. Dave was able to track down extensive information on the car using the VIN number and *www.carfax.com*. Not only did he contact the dealership where the Lexus was initially sold (and read the records of all oil changes and maintenance records), but also with a little online ingenuity he actually tracked down the original owner and asked about the car's history.

- Calculate the costs of transporting the car to your home. Will you have to ship the vehicle or take time off work to drive it home a few hundred (or thousand) miles?

When looking for a used car, newspapers and online sites are excellent resources for comparing prices and shopping for different car models. The *Auto Trader* magazines are another good choice. If you're calling or e-mailing someone about a used car, here are a few questions to include:

- How long have you owned the car? Were you the original owner?

- Do you know if the car has been in any accidents?

- Why are you selling the car?

- Does the car have any mechanical or engineering issues?

- Is there anything on the car, including heat or air conditioner, that doesn't work?

- How many miles are on the car?

- Do you have maintenance records available for review?

If you sense any significant hesitation in the seller's voice, you may have stumbled on an important clue or reason why you should think twice before buying that car. You'll also want to make sure there aren't any liens against the car before you purchase it.

To quickly determine if a car has been through more wear and tear than a seller or dealership is admitting or if the mileage may be higher than the odometer shows, car dealers say there are some easy-to-spot, telltale signs that five-star car buyers should know, including the following:

- There should not be any paint where there is not supposed to be paint. Check the moldings on the car for signs of paint overspray, color, or drips. If the car has been painted, it has either been wrecked or is rusted.

- Worn pedals are signs of age. Brake pedals, gas pedals, and clutch pedals that are worn through on a "low-mileage" vehicle probably mean that the odometer is not showing the true mileage. If the pedal is worn down, the car has seen a lot of use.

- All four tires on the car should match. If the tires don't even match, any work done on the car may have been slipshod. Mismatched tires is a sign of cutting corners to make a car just look good enough to sell.

- Oil drips anywhere except the valve covers can mean trouble. Oil on the valve cover gaskets is generally inexpensive to repair. Most valve covers leak. Oil leaking from the front main bearing seals and rear main seals can be very expensive to replace.

- Cars more than ten years old are not required to show true mileage. Federal law says cars ten years old and older are exempt from showing accurate mileage, so be aware and informed if you are considering a car that has seen a decade or more of use.

- Missing parts mean shoddy work. Go over the cars you are considering with a fine-tooth comb. Good used vehicles should have all their knobs, buttons, headliners, door seals, and other parts and pieces.

If you prefer going to a single location, you can also buy used cars from car dealerships. Some dealerships offer certified cars, which is a marketing term for "reconditioned." Dealerships have different standards about what "certified" means, so you need to find out specifically what was done to the car to certify it. The car may have just been cleaned up, or it may have been rebuilt from the ground up. Find out what was done. At the same time, you need to check out the buyer's guide sticker that must be posted on every car according to federal law. The guide will tell you if the car has any sort of warranty or if the car is being sold "as is." This is important because some dishonest sales people will tell customers that the car is still under warranty even though the "as is" box is

Live It!
Six Reasons to Walk Off a Car Dealership Lot

1. The salesperson makes you feel uncomfortable.

2. You aren't allowed to test drive the vehicle of your choice.

3. The vehicle is missing a buyer's guide sticker required by federal law.

4. The VIN number on the various parts of the car doesn't match.

5. The seller asks you to pay but can't produce a title immediately.

6. The salesperson refuses to allow you to have a mechanic of your choice check it out.

checked. The unsuspecting customer may drive off the lot with no coverage.

Once you've found the right car, it's time to negotiate. People who sell their own cars may be more or less willing to negotiate based on their financial situation. Dealerships are always willing to negotiate.

Once you have purchased your vehicle, you will need to maintain it. Changing the oil every 3000 miles and having routine maintenance done regularly can add years to the parts on your car and save you money in the long run.

When your vehicle needs a repair, those who want to keep the five-star standard do their homework. Consider the following before agreeing to any repairs:

- Ask for references for a reliable, reasonable mechanic or car repair shop from people you know and trust.

- Know that repairs done at the new car dealerships almost always cost more, but do have your repairs done at the dealership if the car is under warranty.

- Know the terms of your extended warranty, if you have one, and get covered repairs done promptly so as not to run the risk of the warranty expiring before you get around to taking the car in.

- Get only what you need. If you need a tire and the tire shop says you also need $1200 in other repairs, buy the tire only and ask for a written estimate of the other work needed with an item-by-item breakdown. Leave and get other opinions.

- Know that "one-stop shopping" almost always costs more. If you want to have your brakes, clutch, air-conditioning, and transmission repaired all at the same place, it will probably cost more than going to different shops specializing in each of those repairs.

- Know that at 50,000 miles, most cars usually need repairs on major systems. Normally, 50,000 miles is the time to replace timing belts, brake systems, air-conditioning systems, and more. If you are considering a car with 50,000 miles or more, ask how many of these items have already been taken care of.

Big-Ticket Items

★ Before you begin shopping for a home, find out what you can afford, not just the size of the loan they'll give you.

★ When purchasing a home, always consider resale value. Property is one of the prime ways to increase your overall net worth.

★ Always shop around for a mortgage broker and home insurance. Their competitive business nature will save you money.

★ Before furnishing a house, make a budget. Invest larger portions of money into the pieces that you'll use the most and are the most important to you.

★ Always do your homework when it comes to buying a car.

★ Be willing to negotiate with a car salesperson. They expect it.

★ If possible, buy and drive used cars which hold their market value better than new ones.

★ Look for signs that a used car has been wrecked, rusty, or not repaired well.

★ Find out what major repairs have been done already on older used cars with more than 50,000 miles.

★ Maintain your vehicle well, and it will maintain more of its value.

★ Know how to look for oil leaks on used vehicles before you buy.

Giving Big on
Only a Little

There's an undeniable natural thrill in finding a discount and saving money. It's well-known that many Hollywood stars, millionaires, and even billionaires enjoy finding a deal, whether it's on the latest fashion, jewelry, vacations, or real estate. The big difference in spending for the thrill of spending (and mostly for yourself) and a five-star life is that those who enjoy Five-Star Living don't let their excitement end with a register receipt. They allow the joy to continue through what they give, donate, and contribute to others.

The good news is that you don't have to have lots of money to make an impact. Simply by making little cutbacks here and there, you can not only multiply your savings, but also increase the amount that you give. That's the goal of Five-Star Living—to help you find ways to make the most of what you have, enjoy your life to the fullest, and spill over with joy that you can share with others. When you give, it costs you something. But giving gives you far more than it takes. When you give sacrificially, God has room to replace what you have given up. His blessings will knock your socks off as you put others first.

My husband and I have experienced firsthand the joy of giving to those in need, and the blessings we receive are far greater than any dollar amount we contribute. One example for our family is our partnership with Compassion International. We joined Compassion on a trip to a South American country where they have a food-and-education program for children who are living in poverty. The kids live in dirt-floor "homes" constructed of whatever materials can be cobbled together, without the amenities (such as running water in many cases) that I take for granted every day. Compassion feeds the kids daily, helps them with homework, teaches them lessons that range from good hygiene to finding faith, and helps them work toward a better future. As a couple, my husband and I decided to sponsor monthly one of the children in that program. We met her, and now we exchange letters with her through Compassion. She is part of our family, and we are better off for it.

Our kids have joined in by using some of the ten percent of their allowances they are required to give to put toward our sponsored child. They also write to her, and we pray for her together. When we talk about her and the different hardships she faces, it reminds us of just how many blessings we have. The $32 a month we send is less than I spend on one Diet Coke fountain drink each day, my husband spends on his daily coffee, or our 10-year-old son spends on a beloved Game Boy game. Five-Star Living does not necessarily mean that we have to give up all of the creature comforts we are blessed with, but it expands our hearts and helps us reevaluate our priorities.

As a family, you can teach your kids to give of their time and talents in addition to their money. Maybe you would want to participate in a neighborhood cleanup day, a walk-a-thon for an important cause, or hold a fund-raising garage sale for a local family who is adopting or has a special need. Ask your kids for their input and ideas. Their imaginations will take you places you would never have expected, and you will be amazed at their capacity for generosity. Once they are taught how, and they see the joy on someone's face who receives a gift given with love, they tend to give freely and joyfully.

Giving benefits our marriage in unexpected ways too. It binds us in a common purpose, strengthens our relationship as we make decisions of where to give together, and simplifies our life. One of the most exciting aspects of giving is that it frees you from allowing your possessions to possess you. Through giving, you let go of the need to let stuff and things control your life and instead provide a testimony to God's provision. You demonstrate the faith that he will remain faithful in giving to you. Matthew 6:30-33 highlights this truth:

> If God gives such attention to the appearance of wildflowers—most of which are never even seen—don't you think he'll attend to you, take pride in you, do his best for you? What I'm trying to do here is to get you to relax, to not be so preoccupied with getting, so you can respond to God's giving. People who don't know God and the way he works fuss over these things, but you know both God and how he works. Steep your life in God-reality, God-initiative, God-provisions. Don't worry about missing out. You'll find all your everyday human concerns will be met (MSG).

Through giving, you awaken to both the God-initiative and the God-reality that is in your life. Remember that the giving element in a five-star life isn't just about finances. It reaches further into your relationships and involvement in the community. It includes the listening ear you offer to a friend going through a hard time, the moment you patiently wait for an elderly person to cross the street, and the Saturday afternoon volunteering to sort through clothes at the Salvation Army. Five-Star Living means putting your talents and time to work in the directions that God leads, letting him steer you to exciting places and stretch you out of your comfort zone in new directions.

Here are some of our favorite ways to contribute to others:

- Tithe to your local church. By giving ten percent of your income to your local congregation, you are helping support others in the community through your donations. If you haven't started tithing already, begin today.

- Support nonprofit radio and television shows. Do you have a Christian program, either on radio or television, that really encourages you and breathes life into you? If so, consider writing them an encouraging letter, praying for the station and its employees, and making a donation. While you should avoid high-pressure tactics to give, you also need to be sensitive to supporting the outreaches that mean the most to you.

- Sponsor a child. An enriching and potentially life-changing event is choosing to sponsor a child from a third world country. For around a dollar a day, you can help make sure one of the poorest of the poor receives a warm meal and education. Some programs even allow you to visit your child in their native country, a rewarding experience for everyone involved. Consider sponsoring a child through Compassion International, *www.compassion.com,* or World Vision, *www.worldvision.org.*

- Donate your next big hair cut. If you are having more than ten inches cut off your hair, consider donating your clippings to Locks of Love, *www.locksoflove.org.*

The nonprofit organization provides hair pieces to underprivileged children under the age of 18 suffering from long-term hair loss. The company uses hair donations to develop hair prostheses. For more information about how to donate, call (888) 896-1588.

- Mentor someone. If you want to become involved in mentoring or forming a relationship with a child or teen, contact your local chapter of Big Brothers Big Sisters, *www.bbbsa.org.* You can also become a mentor through employer and church programs. But remember that some of the most effective and long-lasting mentoring relationships are built organically on a one-on-one level. Is there a younger married couple who has asked you for advice? Do you have any college students or recent graduates that naturally like to hang out at your home? Look for ways to be intentional about your relationships, and if you don't already have one, look for a mentor for yourself.

- If Election Day is around the corner, consider volunteering at your local polls. Not only will you meet new people, but also you'll help preserve one of our nation's greatest freedoms.

- Minister to someone who is imprisoned. If you don't have time to get involved in a prison outreach such as Prison Fellowship, *www.pfm.org,* then you can still serve children of prisoners through Project Angel Tree. For more information, call (800) 55-ANGEL.

- If you want to make a donation with just a moment of your time, there are several websites you can visit and click and the sponsors or advertisers will make a small donation to a charity. So the next time you're online, visit *www.freedonation.com.* Other sites include *www. thehungersite.com,* *www.thebreastcancersite.com,* *www. thechildhealthsite.com,* *www.theliteracysite.com,* *www.*

theanimalrescuesite.com, and *www.therainforestsite.com.*
Some sites limit you to one click a day, while other
sites allow you several clicks.

- If you want to give the gift of giving, Charity Checks,
  www.charitychecks.us, allows you to purchase checks
  in many denominations and then give them as a gift.
  The gift recipient can choose any nonprofit organization to fill the check out to. This is a great gift that
  keeps giving. You get the tax write-off, your recipient
  gets the satisfaction of helping a person or organization in need, and the charity receives the funds it
  needs.

- Volunteer your time to babysit for a mom in need,
  clean the home of an elderly friend, or put your
  knowledge to work tutoring students or leading a
  Sunday school class or Bible study. Your efforts may
  be just what someone needs.

- Depending on your schedule, you may not be able to
  commit to any large or long-term projects, but you
  can still make a difference. Offer to bake or bring
  treats to a church activity or event. Pick up the trash
  on the side of the road when you're walking. Take
  someone who is involved in full-time outreach or
  ministry out to lunch. Little things do make a big
  difference!

Remember that giving is also contagious. When you get
excited about giving, your efforts multiply. Like a pebble
thrown into a lake, the tiny splash it makes soon creates a
ripple effect that can move the surface of the entire lake. Consider the true stories told in the little books *Kingdom Assignment 1* and *Kingdom Assignment 2.* Author and pastor Denny
Bellesi preached at his Coast Hills Community Church in
Aliso Viejo, California, on the subject of being faithful stew-
ards. He ended the sermon by handing 100 members of the
congregation $100 each. He instructed the recipients that the

money was not theirs but God's, and that they were to invest it to please him. The congregants got excited about helping others and multiplying that money and began charity effort after charity effort. It did not take long before those few hundreds turned into hundreds of thousands of dollars being put to work to transform people's lives. You can do the same. We encourage you to start today.

If you're looking for ways to live better, we hope this book has given you some helpful insights and practical tips to set you on the right path. Embrace the Live It! Give It! principles, and begin truly living a five-star life. You'll be so glad you did!

Giving Big on Only a Little

★ Practice cheerful giving. It's fun to see how you can help others. Happy giving is always contagious. Others will give too.

★ Constantly be on the lookout for new opportunities to give.

★ Get rid of stuff. Too much stuff takes control of your time and energy.

★ Give yourself to those you love. Don't hold back from loving.

★ Mentor a teen or sponsor a needy child.

★ Make a family's Christmas wishes come true.

★ Give more than you usually do.

★ Don't just give your money, but also your time, knowledge, and talents to help those in need,

Five-Star Resources

We want to give you a five-star start to hunting down the great deals we have described as a jumping-off point to discovering your own five-star savings style. Here are the websites, helpful hints, and resources we shared in each chapter, all in one easy place for you to flip through and find so you can be on your way to the five-star life you desire.

Chapter 2: Managing Your Methods
Quicken and Microsoft Money

These money managing software programs allow you to input all of your accounts and expenses; and the program keeps a running track of your debt, expenses, and income by categories, making tax time and budgeting a cinch. They can be ordered and downloaded online or purchased just about anywhere software is sold.

Crown Financial Ministries—www.crown.org; (800) 722-1976

Crown Financial Ministries offers invaluable resources to help you make wise choices with your finances. The website has articles and free online coaching, plus Crown trains budget coaches around the country to work with people to help them budget and get out of debt. The best part: It's absolutely free.

Organize Everything—www.organize-everything.com

Organize Everything offers coupon pouches of different shapes and sizes, along with just about any other product you can think of to help organize your home, office, and closets. One coupon pouch they have for $4.99 velcros to your shopping cart for easy access.

Entertainment Book—www.entertainment.com

The Entertainment company prints annual coupon books for different metropolitan areas around the country that cost $20 to $25. The books contain special offers from restaurants, grocery stores, movie theaters, dry cleaners, and much more.

Samaritans Purse, Operation Christmas Child—www. samaritanspurse.org

The Operation Christmas Child program by Samaritan's Purse sends shoeboxes filled with health and beauty items, toys, school supplies, and other items to children in need around the world.

Your Local Newspaper—Sunday Edition

The Sunday paper is the best source for coupons. Buy it only on Sundays, get a subscription, or stop by your local newspaper office on Monday mornings and ask for leftover coupon inserts.

Chapter 3: Beauty Bargains and Fashion Flair
Dress for Success—www.dressforsuccess.org

Dress for Success takes donated professional women's attire and gives the clothes to low-income women who desire to transition into the workforce. It's a great way to clean out your closet and help someone feel her best at her interviews and new job.

Off-Season Shopping

If you can wait for that oh-so-trendy, whatever-your-heart-desires item, you can buy it at the end of the season with considerable savings of 50 percent or more.

Department Stores and Boutique Clearance Racks—Head for the Back

High-end department stores and glamorous boutiques generally put their marked-down items on racks in the back of the store or department. Make it a habit to bypass all the great stuff in the front and head for the back first.

Filene's—www.filenesbasement.com

Filene's has famous discount stores called Filene's Basement in Atlanta, Boston, Washington, DC, and New York City.

Luxe—www.luxeatlanta.com

Luxe is a 5000-square-foot store in the Buckhead area of Atlanta that features so-last-season designer clothes at 50 to 85 percent off the original retail price.

Name Brand Clothing—www.nbcclothing.com

In the Midwest states of Oklahoma, Texas, Arkansas, Missouri, Kansas, and Nebraska, the NBC chain, also known as Name Brand Clothing, warehouses literally tons of off-season and slightly damaged clothing and accessories at rock-bottom prices.

Bluefly and Designer Outlet—www.bluefly.com and www.designeroutlet.com

These websites offer discounts on couture clothes and accessories. A recent Helen Wang pink brocade rounded collar blazer was $239.20 on Bluefly—marked down from $500. An Armani velvet scarf was priced at $75 at Designer Outlet—reduced from $180. Both offered more than 50 percent savings on the original retail price.

Chelsea Premium Outlet Malls—www.premiumoutlets.com

Chelsea Premium Outlets chain, with locations from Orlando to Los Angeles and from Seattle to Boston, contain stores like Barneys, Escada, Hugo Boss, BCBG Max Azria, Oilily, Burberry, and Ralph Lauren. Register on their website and you can enter the online "VIP Lounge" page, where you can print coupons and look for special events and savings.

Bag Borrow or Steal—www.bagborroworsteal.com

At Bag Borrow or Steal, for a monthly fee ranging between $19.95 to $149.95, you can choose one of three main levels of membership (Trendsetter, Princess, or Diva), which will give you access to borrowing the latest brands and styles of Coach, Fendi, and other designer bags.

Jemznjewels—www.jemznjewels.com

Visit Jemznjewels for gently used jewelry from companies like Tiffany & Co. and designer watches from companies like Bedat.

Consignment Stores and Thrift Stores

If gently used items are not your idea of Five-Star Living, skip this pointer; but if you don't mind picking up something that once belonged to someone else, consignment boutiques and thrift stores can offer great discounts on designer items.

Christabelle's Closet—www.christabellescloset.com

If you can't find a consignment shop near your home, visit an online fashion resale store like www.christabellescloset.com. The site recently featured a pair of Prada Mary Janes for $80.

Department Store Cosmetics—Look for Holiday Deals

Stock up on your makeup and perfumes before Christmas and around Mother's Day and Father's Day for the best deals on gift packages, free bonus items, and other special offers. Also, ask your favorite department store when your brand will be "in-gift," meaning they offer a free gift with purchase. Estée Lauder, Lancôme, and Clinique regularly offer gift bags filled with products two or three times a year as a gift with purchase.

Your Favorite Beauty Products Online—www.ebay.com, www.froogle.com, www.shopping.com, www.pricegrabber. com, and www.bizrate.com

Thousands of top-brand cosmetics are available on the auction site eBay and other online sites. If you have fallen in love with a $50 cream or makeup item or find that a particular product makes all the difference in your appearance, look for a good deal online. Be sure to calculate in the shipping and handling to see how much savings you really receive.

Three Custom Color Specialists—www.threecustom.com

The New York City-based company has a list of the secret mixes of more than 7500 different lipstick colors and can recreate your favorite if it is discontinued. You simply slip a small slice of your old color into a small bag and mail it to the company. For $50 they'll create two new tubes of your favorite color.

Chapter 4: Terrific Treats for Tots to Tweens

Free Baby Magazine Subscriptions to American Baby and Baby Talk—www.americanbaby.com and www.parenting. com

Ongoing freebies for parents of the tiniest tots include free six-month subscriptions to *American Baby* magazine, a *Better*

Homes & Gardens publication, and *Baby Talk* magazine, a *Parenting* magazine publication.

Ringling Bros. Circus Ticket—www.ringling.com

Ringling Bros. Barnum & Bailey Circus gives babies up to one year a voucher for a free circus ticket to be redeemed anytime during their lifetime. Parents must sign up for the Baby's First Circus voucher online, and they'll receive the coupon in the mail.

Tax Software for After-Market Values

Intuit's ItsDeductible and H&R Block's Deduction Pro software run about $20 each (and are often free with rebate if you purchase a full tax program) and give you the value of your donated items that can add up to savings on your income taxes.

Tutti Bella's Baby Brand-Name Blog—www.whatshotfor tots.blogspot.com

To see what brands are at the top of the list, visit online company Tutti Bella's running blog for brand descriptions and online boutiques.

Rock Star Baby—www.rockstarbaby.de

Rock 'n' roll star Tico Torres of the popular band Bon Jovi helped develop a trendy brand of infant onesies, T-shirts, and sleepers called Rock Star Baby.

Report Card Rewards, Birthday Freebies, and Summer Reading Rewards

Check with local fun centers, game rooms, fast-food restaurants, party goods stores, and ice-cream shops for report card reward programs and birthday clubs. Many offer free tokens, kids' meals, ice-cream cones, or free items for making good grades and on your child's birthday. Some of our favorite participants include Limited Too, Krispy Kreme, Chuck E. Cheese, and Blockbuster. Summer reading programs from Barnes & Noble and Pizza Hut have offered free books and pizza and drinks for kids who read a certain number of books.

Old-Fashioned Treats—eBulkCandy, www.ebulkcandy.com, and Sweet Nostalgia, www.sweetnostalgia.com

You can introduce your kids to your favorite treats of the past by offering them some BB Bats, MoonPies, SweetTarts, Dots, wax bottles, or striped candy sticks. Grab some at Cracker Barrel restaurants, eBulkCandy, or Sweet Nostalgia. EBulk offers three-pound assortments of "decade" candy for less than $30. You can choose from pre-1950s, 1950s, 1960s, or 1970s.

Family Fun Magazine—www.familyfun.go.com

Family Fun offers illustrated step-by-step instructions for fantastic cakes from dinosaurs to mermaids. This magazine is also a wealth of resources for family activities, party planning, and easy arts and crafts.

Coolest Kid Birthday Parties—www.coolest-kid-birthday parties.com

Another awesome site for party ideas and step-by-step directions is Coolest Kid Birthday Parties, which includes pictures and directions for Hummer cakes, pirate cakes, Barbie cakes, and just about any other kind of cakes, as well as theme ideas, decorations, activities, and printable invitations.

Kids Eat Free—www.kidseatfree.com

This site lists restaurants state by state that offer free kids meals with adult purchase.

Chapter 5: Gourmet Groceries and Decadent Dining

Grocery Store Member Cards—Albertsons, Winn Dixie, CVS, and more

Some grocery and drug stores offer member cards that give you access to special deals each week. Keep in mind that, in exchange for the discounts, you are trading your contact information and spending habits.

UPromise—www.upromise.com

UPromise is a website that offers "rebates" for shopping at participating stores and online retailers. The rebates are put into an online account for your kids to use for college. By registering your grocery store cards and credit cards, your purchases are tracked and a small percentage is returned to you as a college fund.

Online Grocery Coupons—Cool Savings, www.coolsavings. com, and SmartSource Coupons, www.smartsource.com.

Many product coupons can be printed off the Internet. Check out sites like Cool Savings and SmartSource Coupons for extra savings.

Rebate Supplies

In order to take advantage of rebate offers, keep scissors, envelopes, pens, and stamps in one place. Have a small copier available, and keep receipts in a basket or box. Fill out rebate slips and pull together UPC codes and receipts as soon as you get home from the store.

Trader Joes—www.traderjoes.com

Trader Joes offers good prices and occasional great discounts on an assortment of gourmet goodies. You will find all kinds of hard-to-find sweets and treats as well as coffees, teas, gourmet pastas, sauces, and other food items.

Gourmet Treats—Froogle, www.froogle.com, and Epicurean Foods, www.epicureanfoods.com

You can find deals on all kinds of gourmet treats at Froogle and Epicurean Foods, plus many other online sources.

Free Daily Recipes—Food Network, www.foodnetwork.com, and Daily Message, www.dailymessage.com/recipe.shtml

Several sites offer to deliver recipes via email. Subscriptions are free.

Meals of the Rich and Famous

Consider buying a cookbook penned by the chef of a famous person. For example, if you ever wanted to dine at the White House, then you might want to consider the cookbook *Dessert University* (Simon & Schuster, $40) by Roland Mesnier, who served as the pastry chef for the White House for more than 25 years.

Restaurant Recipes to Try at Home—Copykat, www.copykat.com, and Top Secret Recipes, www.topsecretrecipes.com

You can find recipes for many restaurant favorites online at Copykat and Top Secret Recipes. On these sites, you can find recipes for Olive Garden Stuffed Mushrooms and Planet Hollywood's Potstickers, plus hundreds more.

Morris Press Cookbooks—www.morriscookbooks.com

For true five-star cooking, preserve your family's history and your favorite memories by creating a personalized family cookbook. Morris Press Cookbooks allows each family member to go online and input recipes. The company then assembles the recipes into a softcover, hardback, or three-ring cookbook, complete with dividers, pictures, and even family history, depending on which package you choose, for under $5 each.

iDine—www.idine.com

If you like earning airline miles, then you should see if your credit card is linked into the iDine promotion, a program which allows you to earn extra miles based on the restaurants you enjoy.

Chapter 6: Let Us Entertain You

Association of Science-Technology Centers—astc.org

This website will help you find great admission rates to participating science centers.

National Park Service—www.nps.gov/volunteer

Through their website, the National Park Service looks for volunteers. A few of the positions even include food, housing, or transportation reimbursement.

Broadway Show Tickets

You can find reduced last-minute tickets to Broadway shows at the TKTS booth in the center of Times Square. If you want to buy in advance, consider joining organizations such as Audience Extras (AE), Play by Play, and Theatermania.com's Gold Club. You may have to pay an annual membership fee, but you'll be given offers on reduced price Broadway and Off-Broadway shows. Also check out *www.playbill.com*.

Chapter 7: The World As Your Oyster

Priceline—www.priceline.com

This travel auction site allows you to try to bid any price you want for airline flights, hotels, car rentals, and vacation packages. If you're flexible about your arrival and departure times, there's usually no better place than Priceline.

Bidding for Travel—www.biddingfortravel.com

Bidding for Travel is an independent site designed specifically to help give Priceline shoppers bidding strategy. Message boards contain information on recently accepted bids, counteroffers, and prices on various travel itineraries.

Hotwire—www.hotwire.com

A great alternative bidding website.

Seat Expert and Seat Guru—www.seatexpert.com and www.seatguru.com

Tired of being crunched in a middle seat for a four-hour cross-country flight? You can find the best seats at these two websites, which help you identify the most comfortable seats on an aircraft.

Terrific Travel Deals

Cheap Tickets, *www.cheaptickets.com*; Lowest Fare, *www.low estfare.com*; Yahoo, *www.travel.yahoo.com*; Star Travel, *www. startravel.com*; Cheap Seats Travel, *www.cheapseatstravel.com*; Orbitz, *www.orbitz.com*; SideStep, *www.sidestep.com*; Lowest Air Price, *www.lowestairprice.com*; Travelocity, *www.travelocity. com*; Expedia, *www.expedia.com*; and Qixo, *www.qixo.com*.

Fly Share—www.flyshare.com

Private pilots look for people to share the expense of a private flight. It can be difficult to match up itineraries, but you never know when a private pilot may be headed in the right direction. Just be sure to ask about the person's flight record!

Frequent Flyer Programs

Almost every airline offers frequent flyer mile programs, and they are worth the effort. Before you fly, check your airline's partners to see which membership number you should enter before your next flight to receive the most miles.

Hotel Deals—Qixo, www.qixo.com, Quikbook, www. quikbook.com, and others

Two often overlooked, but highly valuable sites when it comes to finding a hotel deal are *www.qixo.com* and *www.quik book.com*. Other sites worth visiting include *www.booking buddy.com*, *www.cheapflights.com*, *www.sidestep.com*, and *www. kayak.com*. They allow you to learn about your hotel and all of the amenities before you make a payment.

SkyAuction—www.skyauction.com

When you're looking for a place to stay, a top site that shouldn't be missed is SkyAuction. The website allows you to bid on travel packages as well as individual airline tickets, hotels, and rental cars. You need to read the fine print as to any extra charges including the fee the website tags onto the cost, but you can find some incredible deals. SkyAuction allows bidders to compete for unsold time-share rentals, airline tickets, and cruises at sometimes ridiculously low prices.

Traveling Solo—Travel Chums, www.travelchums.com, Singles Travel International, www.singlestravelintl.com, and Solo Travel Network, www.cstn.org

Every solo traveler knows about the single-supplement fee. Rather than cut the fare in half, they add a surcharge to the single rate. To avoid these surcharges, consider visiting a travel matching website.

Trip Advisor—www.tripadvisor.com

Check out Trip Advisor before you book any hotel room to read reviews from people who have just stayed there. It can help you avoid hotels with substandard service, rooms, or amenities.

Home Exchange—www.homeexchange.com

If you feel comfortable having strangers in your home, you can participate in a home exchange or a hospitality exchange. For a reasonable fee, a home exchange allows you to travel to exotic homes in places such as the Caribbean and Europe while your home exchange partner stays in your home. In a hospitality exchange, you host each other in your homes at designated times.

Unclaimed Baggage Center—www.unclaimedbaggage.com

The Unclaimed Baggage Center in Scottsboro, Alabama, offers all kinds of luggage and all kinds of items people have left behind on airlines for 30 to 80 percent off.

Time-share Rentals—iVacation, www.ivacation.com, and My Resort Network, www.myresortnetwork.com, Tug 2, www.tug2.net

These sites offer time-share rentals at properties all over the place. Check out Orange Lake Country Club or Bonnet Creek Resort in Kissimmee, Florida, for example. These gorgeous condos and villas can be rented for $500 a week and up, giving you the vacation benefit of a kitchen, planned activities, pools, and other luxuries.

Cruises Only—www.cruisesonly.com

Cruises Only is a great site for searching through all the worldwide cruise lines and destinations for the five-star cruise for you.

Luxury Link—www.luxurylink.com

For high-end and one-of-a-kind vacation packages all over the world, check out Luxury Link. It offers everything from dinners and weekend stays at luxurious restaurants and up-scale hotels in New York City to exclusive winery tours in France.

Centers for Disease Control and Prevention—www.cdc. gov/travel

Check out this site for vaccination recommendations before you go.

Eurail—www.raileurope.com

The Eurail pass entitles you to ride the high-speed trains from country to country at one price.

Best International Travel Deals and Advice—Sidestep, www.sidestep.com

There are hundreds of thousands of Internet blogs, chat sites, and travel sites that can answer your travel questions for any-where around the world—from what to pack to where to eat to the most efficient way to get through customs checks. Try down-loading Sidestep, the international travel search engine software, for instant comparisons of deals offered around the world.

Chapter 8: Entering the High-Tech World

The Computer for Schools Association—www. pcsforschools.org

This organization takes the computer equipment you donate and refurbishes it for use at schools, correctional facilities, and nonprofit organizations. Depending on your location, pickups can be arranged.

Extended Warranties

When buying electronic items, try to buy them from a company or store that offers a good extended warranty policy at a reasonable price. Extended warranties can save you thousands of dollars on big-ticket electronic equipment. On older equipment (such as microwaves and dryers), be careful not to spend more on the warranty than a new replacement would cost.

Wi-Fi—T-Mobile, www.tmobile.com/hotspot

If you need the Internet and don't want to pay for dial-up service, T-Mobile is developing the largest visible number of Wi-Fi "hotspots" in the country, providing access to the Internet for a fee from most Starbucks locations and many airports. The service can be purchased hourly, daily, or monthly for use in any T-Mobile HotSpots.

Free Wireless On-the-Go—Panera restaurants; JWire, www.jwire.com

Panera restaurants nationwide offer free Internet access. You can also find a comprehensive listing of wireless hotspots (free and fee-based) around the country at JWire. Check it before you go on your next trip, and you can find places to plug in and log in that don't cost you a penny.

Donate a Phone Call to Protect—www.wirelessfoundation.org

Donate your old cellular phones to help fight domestic violence. This organization distributes to victims reprogrammed cellular phones with emergency numbers.

Information Without a Fee—Yellow Pages, www.yellowpages.com; White Pages, www.whitepages.com; Switchboard, www.switchboard.com; and Anywho, www.anywho.com

To avoid the excess charges accompanied with dialing 411, use the Internet to track down phone numbers. If you're trying to find an 800 number, call (800) 555-1212. It's a free listing of 800 numbers around the country.

VoIP (Phone Service Through the Internet)—Skype, www. skype.net

One of the best VoIP services is through Skype. It allows you to download software called Softphone that enables you to call two dozen countries for a couple of cents a minute. Other companies including AT&T, Vonage, and Verizon also offer VoIP plans.

Free E-mail Accounts—Yahoo, www.yahoo.com, and Hotmail, www.hotmail.com

Free e-mail accounts abound on the Internet, including those from Yahoo, Hotmail, and GMail, to name a few.

Cell Phone Minute Advisor—Minute Guard, www.minute guard.com

This helpful service sends you a message when you're about to go over your monthly allotment of cell phone minutes.

Satellite Radio—XM, www.xm.com, and Sirius, www.sirius. com

XM and Sirius are the two main competitors for satellite radio service. Both offer more than 100 channels of music for less than $15 a month. Special satellite radio receivers must also be purchased, but they now make ones that can be transferred from car to home.

Woot—www.woot.com

If electronic items are your favorite thing, visit Woot every morning for a special treat. Each day they post quantities of one product at an incredible deal.

Property Room—www.propertyroom.com.

This website is run by Property Bureau, a California company that uses the site to sell items from the property rooms of 425 police and sheriff's departments in 30 states. You can find all kinds of items up for auction, including computers, stereos, and various electronics, at bargain-basement prices.

Kitchen Collection—www.kitchencollection.com

A website for finding new and refurbished kitchen goods.

BizRate—www.bizrate.com

BizRate shows the best prices on electronic and thousands of other items available on the Web. Search for a product, and BizRate will show you the best prices found online. You then follow the link to the site where that price can be found.

Chapter 9: Big-Ticket Items

St. Jude Children's Research Hospital Dream Home Giveaway—www.stjude.org

St. Jude's raffles off homes in cities around the country every year. The houses are valued between $200,000 and $500,000, and tickets are $100 each. There is a maximum of 10,000 tickets sold for each home.

IKEA—www.ikea.com

Ikea offers popular, modern furniture designed to be adaptable and long-lasting.

Craig's List—www.craigslist.com

Craig's List connects buyers and sellers in a given region. You can find all kinds of secondhand furniture, sporting equipment, and appliances. Available in cities around the country, Craig's List offers users the benefit of connecting with other local users to actually see the item before you buy.

Consumer Reports—www.consumerreports.org

When it comes to reviewing cars, *Consumer Reports* is a good guide. Their annual review of automobiles highlights the strengths and weaknesses of a variety of models.

Kelley Blue Book—www.kbb.com

Kelley Blue Book tells you the average value of a given automobile.

Edmunds—www.edmunds.com

Edmunds has developed its own resource for car buyers called *True Market Value* (TMV) pricing. The pricing system is based on actual sales figures, derived from the average price that buyers are paying for a vehicle in your area. It's a handy reference when you're pricing a vehicle.

Fighting Chance—www.fightingchance.com

To find out what a car is really selling for, this fee-based site gives the latest pricing on new vehicles, so you know the true price before you make an offer.

Car Insurance Quotes—Geico, www.geico.com, and Progressive, www.progressive.com

Before buying a car, get insurance rate quotes from several places. You just might be surprised in the insurance price difference between different years, makes, and models.

eBay Motors and Auto Traders—www.ebaymotors.com and www.autotraders.com

These sites will help you find great deals on vehicles.

Carfax—www.carfax.com

Find out all the gritty details on the car you want to buy.

Chapter 10: Giving Big on Only a Little

Child Sponsorship—Compassion International, www.compassion.com, and World Vision, www.worldvision.org

For around a dollar a day, you can help make sure one of the poorest of the poor receives a warm meal and education.

Some programs even allow you to visit your child in their native country, a rewarding experience for everyone involved.

Locks of Love—www.locksoflove.org; (888) 896-1588.

If you are having more than ten inches cut off your hair, consider donating your clippings to Locks of Love. The nonprofit organization provides hairpieces to underprivileged children under the age of 18 suffering from long-term hair loss.

Big Brothers Big Sisters—www.bbbsa.org

If you want to become involved in mentoring or forming a relationship with a child or teen, contact your local chapter of Big Brothers Big Sisters.

Prison Fellowship—www.pfm.org; (800)55-ANGEL(552-6435)

If you want to minister to someone who is imprisoned, get involved in a prison outreach such as Prison Fellowship. You can also serve children of prisoners through Project Angel Tree.

Click-n-Give—Online Donation Sites

If you want to make a donation with just a moment of your time, there are several websites you can visit and click and the sponsors or advertisers will make a small donation to a charity. Visit *www.freedonation.com*, *www.thehungersite.com*, *www.thebreastcancersite.com, www.thechildhealthsite.com, www. therainforestsite.com, www.theliteracysite.com*, and *www.theani malrescuesite.com.* Some sites limit you to one click a day, while other sites allow you several clicks.

Charity Checks—www.charitychecks.us

If you want to give the gift of giving, Charity Checks allows you to purchase checks in many denominations to then give as gifts. The recipients can choose any nonprofit organization to fill the check out to.

About the Authors

Margaret Feinberg (*www.margaretfeinberg.com*) is an award-winning journalist, speaker, and writer. She is the author of more than a dozen books including *Simple Acts of Faith, Just Married,* and *Twentysomething: Surviving & Thriving in the Real World.* Margaret and her husband, Leif, live in Juneau, Alaska, where she loves hiking, kayaking, and chasing the northern lights. During the long dark winters, she's been known to become addicted to reruns of *Law & Order, CSI,* and anything related to reality television.

Natalie Nichols Gillespie (*www.natalienicholsgillespie.com*) is a mom and stepmom of seven who enjoys shopping, reading, and staying in five-star time-shares for only $30 a night! She is the author of *The Stepfamily Survival Guide, 101 Ways to Find God's Purpose for Your Life,* and the "Instant Messages from God" series for teens and kids and has written countless articles for more than 20 magazines and newspapers around the country. Natalie lives with her family in Weeki Wachee, Florida, home of the mermaids.

Do you have your own five-star ideas and tips? If so, we'd love to hear from you! Please e-mail your ideas to *Margaret@ margaretfeinberg.com.*